948 CHU

Chubb, Thomas Caldecott.
The Northmen.

TITLE

DATE DUE                BORROWER'S NAME

948 CHU

Chubb, Thomas Caldecott.          /07
The Northmen.

# The Northmen

OTHER BOOKS ABOUT MAJOR CULTURES OF THE WORLD

ILLUSTRATED BY *Richard M. Powers*

# The Northmen

THOMAS CALDECOT CHUBB

The World Publishing Company · Cleveland and New York

To Mary Alice Victoria Chubb,
on the spinnaker sheet or at the tiller
herself *vikingr mikill*

*Published by* The World Publishing Company
2231 West 110th Street, Cleveland 2, Ohio

*Published simultaneously in Canada by*
Nelson, Foster & Scott Ltd.

Library of Congress Catalog Card Number: 64–12355

# Contents

# Winged Hats at the Holy Island

As the eighth century of the Christian Era drew toward its close, Europe was as peaceful and tranquil as was possible in those turbulent Dark Age days.

The barbarian invasions had just about spent themselves, and indeed many people thought that there were no more barbarians to come. They had been like a plague of locusts. Beginning in 376 A.D., when 200,000 Visigoths defeated and slew a Roman emperor and then poured into the Balkans, horde after horde had crossed either the mighty Danube or the swift and beautiful Rhine. They had fanned out into the dying Roman Empire, spreading wrack and ruin as they went.

Some were from the fens and from the tall oak forests of ancient Germany. These included the Alans, the Alamanni, the Burgundians, the Vandals, the Visigoths, and the Ostrogoths (who had recently moved to the shores of the Black Sea and thus invaded the Roman Empire from the east), the

9

Lombards, and the "free people," or Franks. According to the great Roman historian Tacitus, all of them had "fierce blue eyes, red hair, and huge frames." All, too, were mighty warriors. "They think it stupid to acquire by the sweat of toil what they might win by their blood," he wrote.

Other barbarians had come from the far-distant steppes—from Asia. These were short men, bowlegged from years of horsemanship. They had slant eyes, black stringy hair, and yellowish complexions. They rode small swift ponies, drank fermented mare's milk, and lived in felt tents. Among them were the Avars and the terrible Huns.

The first mortal blow was struck in 410. Alaric, king of the Visigoths, sacked Rome itself. In 455, the Vandals also sacked it. They tore down its aqueducts and wrought such havoc that "vandalism" has been our word for wanton destruction ever since. Then in 476, Odoacer, another blond northern chieftain, deposed Romulus Augustulus, the last Roman emperor, and exiled him to a pleasant villa near Naples. Odoacer proclaimed himself King of Italy. This was the end of the Western Roman Empire. From then on, anarchy and disorder reigned.

But now new kingdoms were arising—and at least one new empire, Frankland or France.

In 768, a tall, handsome, intelligent, athletic young man mounted the Frankish throne. In his own language—for he spoke German—he was Karl der Grosse, but we know him as Charlemagne, or Charles the Great. At that time, the Franks were feeble and divided, but by the time he died he ruled all the lands which today are known as West Germany, Holland, Belgium, and France. He also ruled eastern Austria, Italy almost as far south as Naples, and parts of northern Spain. In 800 he was crowned Emperor of the Romans.

He brought law and order to three fourths of western

Europe—and culture and learning too, for although he himself, try though he did, could not learn to read or write, he assembled the best scholars of the age in his capital city of Aix-la-Chapelle.

South Italy was ruled by the Duke of Spoleto. His dukedom was not a great power, but secure in his mountain fortress he was at least strong enough to defend his seacoasts and sometimes his inland cities from Saracen pirates.

The Byzantine Empire, which at that time extended from Sicily and Sardinia to the eastern boundaries of modern Turkey, was strong and solid. As the eighth century was drawing to its close this empire was ruled first by Constantine Born-in-the-Purple, a learned man whose books on government are still read, and then by Irene, a wicked old lady who was a match for any male ruler there had ever been. They too preserved law and order.

Spain—except for its northwest corner where Christian monarchs still reigned—was now Moorish and ruled by perhaps the strongest rulers in its history. They were tolerant to Christians and to Jews. Culture and industry flourished.

Even England now enjoyed relative tranquillity. As late as 449 it had been a prosperous Roman province, crisscrossed by paved Roman roads, some of which still survive, and filled with handsome Roman villas. But with the fall of Rome, it too had been invaded by the barbarians who dwelt along its borders:

The Picts, or "painted ones," called this because their faces were stained with bright blue woad. These were the "little people" who lived amid the heather of the Scottish Highlands. We get our word "pixie" from them.

The Scots. Actually these were wild Irishmen who only recently had crossed the North Channel of the Irish Sea to settle in the Lowlands.

The fierce Celtic Brigantes. They had always lived in Britain but had never adopted Roman customs or yielded to Roman power.

One of Britain's local kings, Vortigern, concluded that he feared the Saxons, who lived across the North Sea and who had been raiding from time to time as had their neighbors the Angles and Jutes, less than he did the Picts, the Scots, and the Brigantes. He sent emissaries to the homelands of these three tribes near the mouth of the Elbe River and in southern and western Denmark. There, far up a narrow inlet, they found the brothers Hengist and Horsa seated at the ale board.

"Come to Britain, and if you drive off King Vortigern's foes, he will give you wide domains."

Come to that land of fertile soil, rich plowlands, and game-filled forests!

"They landed," says the *Anglo-Saxon Chronicle,* "at Ype-swinesfleot [Ebbsfleet, not far from Dover] at first to help the Britons, but later they fought against them."

Horsa was slain.

Then the dam burst. First to avenge Horsa, but later to win land, Angle and Saxon and Jute poured into the country in their shallow-draft, broad-beamed boats. The Britons fought bravely under such Roman-trained leaders as Ambrosius and Arturius (who was transformed into the legendary King Arthur), but it was useless.

Plumes of black smoke rose from burning edifices. The livestock was butchered. Bridges were torn down or allowed to fall into ruin. The temples and amphitheaters now stabled Saxon or Jute horses. Waterfowl nested in the reed-choked pools of once luxurious baths. The civilization of the Roman-Britons disappeared.

It was replaced by an Anglo-Saxon civilization.

Not too long ago there had been consuls and proconsuls and even little emperors—for at least once Britain had had its own Roman emperor—but they had now vanished. In their place were petty kings, petty queens, thegns (thanes), high reeves, and ealdormen (aldermen) with harsh-sounding names like Beohtric, Ceawlin (Colin), Cwichelm, Eorcenbehrt, and Waebhern.

With the Romans, stone houses disappeared too, and even a city as important as Londinium became little more than a market place. And not a single Anglo-Saxon is known to have moved into a Roman villa!

But in the countryside it was another matter. There the newcomers built up a system of rural townships surrounded by open fields. These townships were really big farms. As in the nursery rhyme, "oats, pease, beans, and barley" were grown. In the adjacent forests, swine fattened upon acorns to become English bacon. In the cleared meadows, *cealf* became *cu* (cow) and provided milk, butter, cheese, and flesh.

At this time, England became Christian too.

Roman Britain was largely pagan, but soon after the Angles, Saxons, and Jutes had established themselves in Somerset and Dorset in southern England, and in Mercia and Northumberland farther north, they adopted the new faith.

The famous monk Augustine landed in Kent, having been sent by Pope Gregory the Great.

Gregory had once seen golden-haired English children in a slave market. "They are angels, not Angles!" he cried. He decided to make them Christian.

The holy Columba, an Irish missionary, crossed the sea to Scotland in a leather-covered coracle, a small craft as flimsy as a kayak. Between them, Augustine and the Irish saint converted both England and southern Scotland.

It was at these Christian, prosperous Anglo-Saxon farmers that a new wave of heathen invaders suddenly struck.

They too came across the chill North Sea.

One of the most famous monasteries in England at this time was Lindisfarne on the island of the same name, which was also known as the Holy Island because of the many saints who had dwelt there.

It lay not more than a dozen miles south of the present-day Scottish border. Separated from the mainland by three miles of mudflats which could be crossed only at low tide and not always then; small—its area was only 1,000 acres—low and dreary; inhabited only by sea birds, it was a place for lonely contemplation. For that reason, there had gathered upon it a company of perhaps three hundred monks.

They lived in humble houses made of sawed oaken timbers covered with thatch and wattles. Even their church, though more impressive, was made of the same materials, which had been transported in carts across the causeway.

There, all winter long, they toiled at manuscripts of incredible beauty. Some of them were illuminated manuscripts almost as lovely as the famous *Book of Kells* which you can see still in Dublin.

They grumbled as they did so. "I am very cold," wrote one monk. "New parchment. Bad ink. I say no more," wrote another.

In springtime, they planted their gardens.

When summer came, they filled their knapsacks with lowly fare, put on their robes and sandals, and crossed to the main-land. They set off across the hills. There, sleeping in the open or in crofts, and drinking the clear water of Highland streams, they carried the Christian story to the most distant of the Scottish clansmen. All men loved them as they did this. Even the savage—but no longer painted—Picts had a welcome for them and gave them oatmeal and the flesh of deer.

But in June, 793, as they were preparing to go out upon the road, one of the monks looked to the northeast.

"Sails!" he cried. "Sails! Many of them!"

Indeed, there were sails—sails of every color, although most of them were striped red and yellow. And beneath the sails, the rush and beat of oars that stirred the gray North Sea into white whirlpools.

This was a new kind of ship, a new and terrifying kind of ship not ever seen at the Holy Island before. The hulls were long and slender, some painted black, others blood-colored and menacing. As they drew nearer, you could see the sunlight flash on battle-ax, spear, and sword. You could see winged helmets. You could see the metal glint of chain mail byrnies.

As the monks quaked and shook, running this way and that in their terror, the gap of water narrowed until prows grated on the shore, and the men who had crowded the gunwales waded to dry land.

Then suddenly there was nothing but harsh cries to heathen gods and goddesses, and the screaming of men who were chopped or cut to pieces by the marauders who had come storming over the waves. After that the crackle and roar of flames. Every building on Lindisfarne was set on fire. But not until such treasures as were there had been seized and put into pirate holds. The golden chalices. The churchly robes. Even some of the manuscripts.

Then just as they had come, the winged hats scrambled

onto their ships. They pushed them from the beach and sailed off.

There was not a living human being left upon the island.

I have said that Lindisfarne was a refuge for sea birds. The auk nested there, the pintail, the skua, the scoter, the merganser, the cormorant, the eider duck, and the shell duck. These alone wheeled along a deserted shore as dusk fell upon a lovely June evening while the oyster catcher and all kinds of sandpipers circled just above the waves and hopped daintily along the shore.

# The Creek Men from Scandinavia

Almost as the raiders sailed away, a great wave of shock and astonishment swept through most of Europe. It did not take long for Lindisfarne's smoke to drift off and dissolve nor for the red-hot timbers of the burned monastery to cool and crumble into charred ruins. But hardly had this happened before tidings of the disaster spread abroad.

The tinker plodding through the oak forests of England laden with the pots and pans which he would sell to Anglo-Saxon farmers; the merchant who crossed the English Channel in his broad-beamed boat and then moved on to Lyon or Cologne; the churchman slowly making his way toward Rome—all of these told the same story and were asked the same question.

"Who," they were asked, "were these tall strong-armed men who had scrambled waist-deep through the lead-colored surf, killed and burned and pillaged, and then, staggering

18

under their booty, splashed their way back to their ships again? Who were these new barbarians, who, after several centuries of relative peace, now invaded the south once more?"

The men who bore the tidings could not answer.

Neither could the monks of Lindisfarne—those who, by somehow or other crossing to the mainland, had managed to escape being cut down in cold blood. To them—as to the author of an ancient history in which their deeds are described—the raiders were nothing but wicked and gutteral-speaking destroyers who had come and struck without warning and had then "ravaged and laid waste God's holy church, robbing and slaying."

Even Alcuin—the great English scholar, who lived at the court of Charlemagne and tried to teach that monarch to read and write—was hardly more specific.

"Think you!" he exclaimed. "We and our forefathers have dwelt in Britain for more than three hundred fifty years and never has there been such a terror as this pagan marauding! Never did we imagine that there could be such a sailing of ships! Think you! The church of St. Cuthbert bespattered with the gore of its priests and despoiled of its glories! Think you! This place, more revered than any other in the land given over to godless pirates for their plundering!"

"Heathen men."

"Pagan marauding."

"Godless pirates."

That is all that even Alcuin could say about the raiders of Lindisfarne.

But we now know a great deal more about them than that. Heathen men, the weapon-wielding marauders who stepped ashore at Lindisfarne indeed were; and, by Christian standards, they were godless pirates. (We must remember, however, that almost all of our accounts of these pirates' deeds were written by monks who had good reason to be prejudiced.)

But they were heathen men and godless pirates from a special place and of a special sort. They were the famous vikings, or creek men of Scandinavia. ("Men of the *viks,* or creeks," is the probable meaning of the word *viking,* although there are some who say that it comes from the Latin *vicus,* or "village," and others that it comes from the Old English *wicing* which means "warrior.")

They were the people whom today we call the Northmen. A viking was merely a special kind of Northman: a sea-warrior who made his living—or made much of it—from raiding and roving. But the term viking is sometimes used loosely for Northman, since most of the Northmen who appeared in western and southern Europe were vikings.

They were members of the northwestern branch of the great Germanic peoples. Germany, wrote Tacitus, is separated from Gaul (France) and Pannonia (parts of modern Austria and Hungary) by the Rhine and the Danube. Mountains divide it from the Sarmatians and the Dacians, the inhabitants

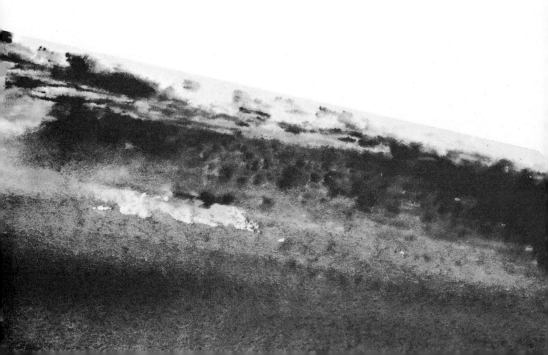

of south Russia and Romania. "Elsewhere," he continued, "oceans gird it, embracing broad peninsulas and islands of unknown extent."

The Northmen were the inhabitants of those broad peninsulas and vast islands. (Denmark is a peninsula, and the ancients, including Tacitus, thought that Norway and Sweden made up a single vast island. Today we call this peninsula and this "island" Scandinavia, and have extended the term to include Iceland.)

They were then, of course, cousins to the other forty or fifty Germanic tribes described by Tacitus and were close cousins

to the Angles, Saxons, and Jutes. Indeed, although he did not mention the Saxons, Tacitus specifically included the Anglii and the Eudoces (Jutes) in a long list of tribes dwelling in Denmark.

These Norse tribesmen, mentioned by Tacitus and by many others, had lived in Scandinavia for a very long time.

Archaeologists say that Scandinavia was inhabited almost as soon as the great glacier of the last Ice Age retreated toward the pole. This could not have been much later than 10,000 B.C.

The first inhabitants were almost certainly hunters who followed the game northward, for what they left behind them, along with some ancient clothing and a little pottery, were largely flint and sometimes reindeer-antler knives and arrowheads and spear points and hide scrapers. Their kitchen middens were filled with bones of elk and aurochs. They may have been nomadic ancestors of the small and swarthy Lapps, or they may have been Basque-like Iberians similar to ones who were moving into the British Isles at about the same time. In either case, they were short of stature and dark.

The blond people who succeeded them and who were the true forebears of the Northmen themselves arrived many thousands of years ago too.

Not later than 2000 B.C. and probably 2500 B.C. or earlier, the Indo-Europeans spread out from their ancestral homeland which was probably near the shores of the Black Sea. At this time their Germanic branch moved into central and western Europe, occupying most of the wide lands that extended from the sand dunes of the North Sea islands to the mouth of the Vistula and thence southward to the mountains that separate Switzerland and Bavaria and Austria from Italy.

Some of them, and in the same dim days, went even farther.

Certain Germanic tribes moved ahead to the moraines and heath-covered sand of what is now Schleswig-Holstein and Denmark. From there, many of them crossed the Skagerrak and the Kattegat to southern Norway and to southern Sweden.

Many of them stayed there. And in these new lands with their pine forests, their lofty snow-choked fells (moors located in the high mountains), and their many deep fjords, they evolved into a new people. Isolated from the rest of Europe—for a while even the Danes were cut off from their fellow Germanic tribes by a huge wedge of advancing Celts which thrust out from present-day Czechoslovakia to the Atlantic Ocean and finally to the British Isles—they were no longer Germans but Scandinavians. Shaped by this isolation, by the rugged life they were forced to live, and also by a climate which around 500 B.C. turned bitterly cold again, they became the people who have given this book its title, a group of tribes and nations that in many ways were unlike any other people who have burst upon the stage of history. In their impact upon western history, they can only be compared with the "golden-haired" Achaeans who suddenly descended on the Mediterranean, and mingling with the dark people who already lived there, gave us the wonderful civilization of ancient Greece.

To be sure, these Northmen retained many of their Germanic characteristics. Although their hair was more frequently yellow than red, their appearance was usually that of the Germans described by Tacitus. They practiced the old religion of their Germanic ancestors. Like their Germanic ancestors, in their homeland they lived modestly off the land —when they were not fighting, that is. They did a little trading too, but only along the shores of the shallow Baltic.

But their own characteristics were many. Although a

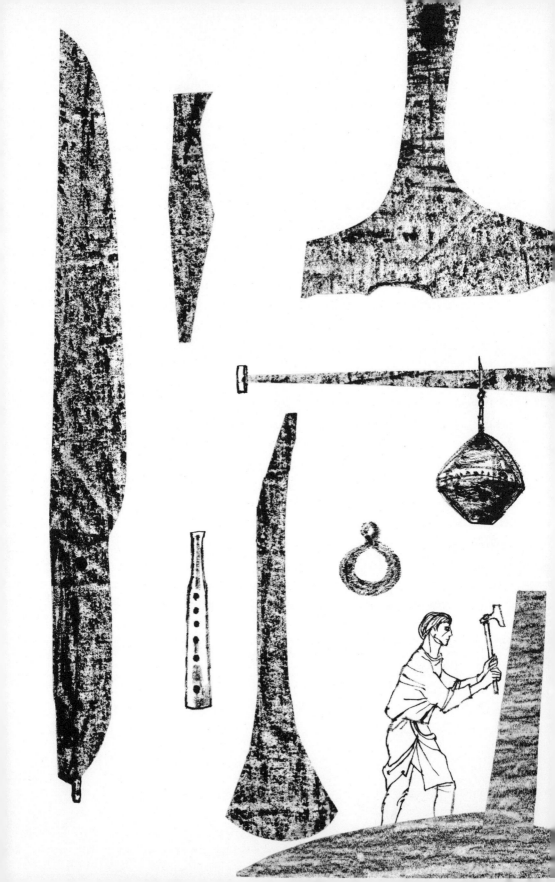

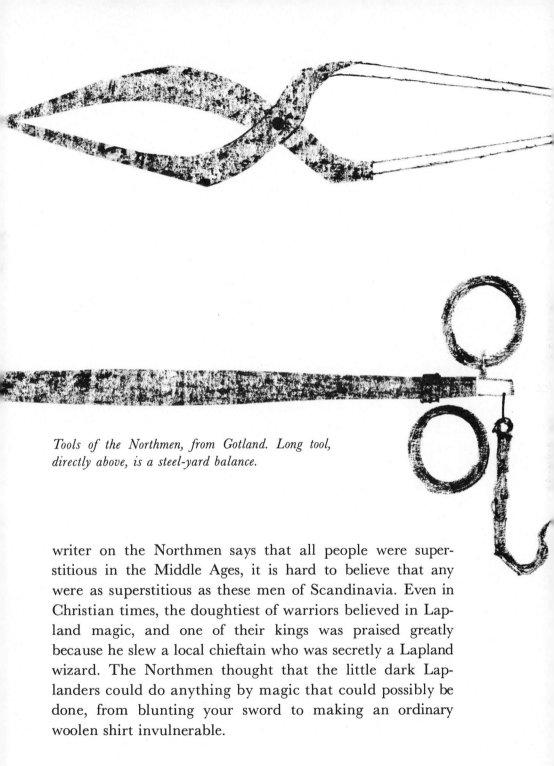

*Tools of the Northmen, from Gotland. Long tool, directly above, is a steel-yard balance.*

writer on the Northmen says that all people were superstitious in the Middle Ages, it is hard to believe that any
were as superstitious as these men of Scandinavia. Even in
Christian times, the doughtiest of warriors believed in Lapland magic, and one of their kings was praised greatly
because he slew a local chieftain who was secretly a Lapland
wizard. The Northmen thought that the little dark Lap-
landers could do anything by magic that could possibly be
done, from blunting your sword to making an ordinary
woolen shirt invulnerable.

The Northmen believed in luck. A man was born lucky or unlucky, and there was nothing you could do about it. They believed in the importance of dreams. They believed that seeing a raven brought good fortune provided it did not croak. They believed that if your horse stumbled as you went into battle, you would either be wounded or slain.

The Northmen believed too that the hills and mountains were filled with trolls, giants, elves, dwarfs, werewolves (men who had changed themselves into wolves), and unipeds. A troll was especially Scandinavian. He was sometimes a giant and sometimes a dwarf, but he was always ugly and he was always evil. Many Norse people believed in trolls almost to modern times.

But the Northmen had noble qualities as well. One of the worst things you could say about a Northman was to call him a *nithing*. *Nithing* means coward, but to the Northmen it meant more than that—it also meant someone "who sneakingly did malicious acts." A man who fled from battle was a *nithing*—but so was a traitor. For although a Northman was quite willing to trick a foe, when he dealt with fellow Northmen he set himself high standards. In many ways, he was a knight errant before his time.

Like a knight errant, the Northman was romantically attached to his weapons. Especially esteemed were swords, many of which were inscribed with runes, the mysterious writing of the ancient Norsemen which was used only for magic and in inscriptions. Most Norse chieftains gave their swords names just as they did their horses and their dogs. "Mill-biter" (because it cut through a millstone) was the name of a sword given to the viking Haakon by King Athelstan of England. "It is the best sword that ever came to Norway!" cried Haakon.

The Northmen were also romantically attached to the sea. They rode their ships as other warriors rode newly broken horses and they were as attached to them as a champion of chivalry was to his prancing steed. When a Norse chieftain died, he was often buried in his ship.

The ships of the Northmen were well worthy of this love and affection. For at the time of their appearance in western Europe, they were the finest vessels man had ever built.

The ancestors of the Northmen had been able shipbuilders even in Roman days.

"The Suiones (Swedes)," wrote Tacitus, "living on the ocean itself have a powerful navy. The form of their vessels is peculiar. They have a prow at either extremity. Hence they are always ready to run into the shore. They are not worked by sails, nor do they have a row of oars permanently attached. Rather the oars can be shifted from side to side."

With this as a prototype, over the course of the years the Northmen gradually developed their own vessel—the famous dragon ship, or long ship.

Actually, of course, the ships of the Northmen were of many sorts. There were ships designed for moving up shallow streams, broad-beamed commercial vessels, and even graceful royal yachts. But the long ship was their warship, and the one most important to us.

A typical long ship was about eighty feet long and had a beam of nineteen feet. It displaced thirty tons, and could clip through the water at a speed of at least 10 knots. It was clinker-built—that is to say, its planks overlapped each other as in a modern sea skiff. Its keel was oak, its ribs beech, and its mast pine. It was caulked with cow hair. Its prow and stern were lofty, and were usually decorated with a gilded dragon head or tail. It had a single square sail, and usually

sixteen pairs of oars which were worked against carved oak posts. On board were two or three small dinghies for landing purposes and sometimes a few portable berths, although usually the crew slept ashore in tents or on the oarsmen's benches when they were at sea. Its normal crew was forty men, but it could carry sixty or seventy. Along its bulwarks hung the round shields, painted black or yellow, of the warriors.

Some long ships, of course, were even bigger than this. One with thirty-four pairs of oars was built, and King Olaf Tryggvason's *Long Serpent* could carry two hundred and fifty men.

They were constructed in great numbers. Indeed, a fleet of from two to three thousand vessels has been recorded. This was probably an exaggeration, but fleets of from thirty to one hundred were frequent, and fleets of more than three hundred have been confirmed.

These viking ships were swifter and more deadly than any other vessel in the world.

It was they that made possible the Viking Age—it has also been called "the heroic age of Scandinavia"—which began at about the time of the attack on the Holy Island and lasted for almost three centuries.

# The Fury of the Northmen

Actually, the attack on Lindisfarne was not the first appearance of these men from the north in England or in the countries to the south of them.

Even as early as 521, for example, Hygelac, king of the Danish Geats—his deeds are described in the Anglo-Saxon poem *Beowulf*—lost his life in a raid against the tribes of what today is Holland.

That was a land attack, of course, but before 700 strange ships, almost certainly bearing Northmen, anchored off the island of Eigg in the Scotch Hebrides and off little Tory Island near Ireland. There were no treasures to seize, but native sheep and scrawny cattle were driven to the beach and butchered.

In 787, other raiders landed in Wessex.

"In those days," says the *Anglo-Saxon Chronicle,* "King Beohtric of Wessex took to wife Eadburgh, daughter of King Offa of Mercia. And at this time came the first three ships of Norwegians. They came from Herethaland." (This is Hördaland in southwest Norway.)

"The king's reeve"—wearing his badges of office, and jogging on a plump well-fed mare—"rode out to meet them, and tried to compel them to go to the royal manor, for he did not know who they were." He was slain by the marauders.

There were undoubtedly other raids and ravages too, but it was not until Lindisfarne that the attacks began in earnest. Then, indeed, "a great sea-cast flood of adventurers"—as one chronicler called them—came out of the mist, and soon they were everywhere.

In 794, the raiders appeared before another monastery, St. Paul's at Jarrow on the mainland near the Scottish Firth of Forth. Here, at least, a viking leader was killed and the invaders driven off. But not until great damage had been done.

In 795, they were in the Hebrides again.

In 798, they came ashore on the Isle of Man. (Its parliament, the Tynwald, has a Norse name and was founded by the vikings.)

In 802, they landed on the island of Iona and destroyed the beehivelike monastery cells St. Columba had built there.

In 835, they were in Cornwall. There they united with the native Britons of Wales and "Bretland," their name for the place, and together did battle with King Egbert and his hated Saxons. Egbert defeated them.

In 840, the ealdorman Wulfheard fought at Southampton against thirty-three ships' companies.

A year later, another ealdorman "was slain by the heathen among the people of Romney Marsh, and in the same year in Lindsey and East Anglia many more men were slain by this host."

In 842, "London was plundered" and in 843, "King Aethelwulf fought thirty-five ships' companies at Carhampton" and the Danes kept possession of the field of battle.

Then, in 851, the Northmen arrived in force, and came to stay. In that year "three hundred fifty ships came to the mouth of the Thames, and stormed Canterbury. They put to flight the King of Mercia."

After that, the Northmen never left Great Britain. That year, they wintered on the flat marshy island of Thanet at the mouth of the Thames where the Britons, the Romans, and the Saxons had first landed. When spring came, they fanned out over the countryside, stealing or buying English horses.

Sometimes they won mighty victories as when they stormed and took Winchester or, having made peace with the Kentishmen, "went secretly by night and devastated all the eastern part of the country." But at other times they were defeated—and "with the greatest slaughter of a heathen host we have ever heard tell of"—as they were by King Ethelwulf and his West Saxon peasants with their homemade weapons and their woolen shirts in a battle on the rolling Downs.

Then in 866—just two hundred years before the Norman conquest—new vikings arrived and the combined forces wintered in East Anglia.

The next year, they marched northward for the first time.

They were bent on revenge as well as conquest, for the leaders of the expedition were three sons of Ragnar Lödbrok (Ragnar Hairybreeches, so called because of the wolfskin trousers stiffened with tar which he always wore with the fur side out).

Some years before, on his way from raids on the continent, Ragnar had been shipwrecked on the English coast, and after a battle with King Aella of Northumbria had been captured and cast into a pit filled with poisonous vipers.

"The porkers would grunt if they knew the fate of the

boar!" he cried as the venomous serpents clung to every part of his body.

Then he laughed, for a viking chieftain must always meet his death scornfully. "Tomorrow I will drink beer with Odin!"

The porkers, Ragnar's sons, did indeed grunt. And they bared their tusks as well.

With their great host they crossed the Humber River and before long, Aella was in their hands. They cruelly put him to death by carving a blood-eagle upon his back; that is, they tore his ribs from his backbone and pulled out his lungs through the gap. It was a favorite viking torture.

With Aella slain, nothing stood in their way, and gathering their forces they marched to York, which they took with immense slaughter. At that time the city got its present name, and this we should remember, for place names and the names of people often tell us much history. The Romans had called it Eboracum. Then the Celts called it Caer Abroc, their way of saying Eboracum City. The Saxons twisted this a little further and called it Eoforwik. Now it became Jorvik, or York. It has been York ever since.

With York in Northman hands, England was divided by treaty into two almost equal parts. The well-drained lowlands north and east of the rivers Thames and Lea and of ancient Watling Street (which ran from Durham to the Cheviot Hills) was called the "Danelaw." It was ruled by the viking Danes. South and west was the Wessex of the West Saxons.

Not too long afterward the island was united again, under the West Saxons, by Alfred the Great and later by his valiant daughter, Aethelflaed, who rode at the head of her troops like a man and who was known as "the Lady of the Mercians."

But in the old Danelaw, Danish influence did not disappear. There are traces of it especially in place names even today.

The sea raiders from Scandinavia poured into Ireland too. But in Ireland there was a different situation. Although the Irish had been converted to Christianity by St. Patrick almost one hundred fifty years before St. Augustine landed in England, and although in Erin Irish monks kept alive a love of beauty and of learning, when it had died almost everywhere else in northern Europe, most of the Irish were still half-naked savages.

They lived hidden in the bogs, speared or netted salmon in their many rivers and deep lakes, and hunted the elk and waterfowl. Politically, they were divided into too many clans to number, and each clan had its own king. To be sure, these clans were supposedly united into five kingdoms and four of the five bowed the knee to the *ardri,* or high king, at Tara. But actually every clan fought every other clan. The result was a confusion that made things easy for the invaders.

The Northmen took advantage of this. In 795, vikings from Norway—the earliest invaders of Ireland were Norwegian— attacked Lambay Island not a dozen miles north of present-day Dublin Bay. In 807 they were marching inland. They crossed half the island.

In 811 they plundered Cork in the far south, and in 827 they destroyed every monastery in northern Ireland.

By 834—says the ancient Irishman who wrote the *Annals of Ulster*—there was not a single part of the Emerald Isle which did not know them.

Fifteen years later, in 849, invaders came from another part of Scandinavia. The *Finngail* ("white foreigners," or Norwegians) were followed by the *Dubbgail* ("black for-eigners," or Danes). Soon Dubbgail was fighting Finngail as furiously as he fought the native Irish, and in one battle the Danes boasted that they had slain five thousand Norwegians. As a thanks offering for their victory, the Danish vikings sent a large chest of gold and silver to honor St. Patrick. Although they were heathen, they saw no harm in calling on a Christian saint.

At this time, liking the country, many who had been raiders became permanent settlers.

Some of the viking chieftains became famous Irish kings. One of these was Thorgils, who around 840 proclaimed himself "king of all the strangers in Ireland." With his wife Aud —one of the two Auds who became renowned in Northman history—he conquered most of the island and then set up his court at Clonmacnoise on the Shannon River. There he levied Danegeld—a tax one had to pay for the right to be left alone—upon the natives and proclaimed himself Abbot of Armagh. He strutted about clad in ecclesiastical finery, while Aud, just to make sure that the Norse gods were not offended, made prophecies and chanted heathen spells from the high altar.

But Thorgils was not content to let things stay at that. He rashly attempted to convert the whole land to his pagan faith, and in so doing came into conflict with one of the few strong Irish kings, Malachy I. In 845, Malachy captured him after a bloody battle and executed him by drowning him in Lake Owel.

Even more famous was Olaf the White. He was a son of Lochlann ("lake land," or Norway), and his wife was the other Irish Aud. This Aud was the daughter of the first Norse chieftain to rule in the Hebrides. Because of her wisdom, she was known as Aud the Deep-Minded.

Olaf ruled for eighteen years with such skill that this time many of the Irish did renounce their baptism and adopt the faith of their conquerors.

These were the so-called Gall-Gaidhels, or "foreign Irish." Some of them were pure-blooded Irishmen, but others were children of marriages between Irish women and viking men. They helped the Northmen hold what they had won, but in their native land they were denounced as wicked-living renegades and traitors. Their broken speech was scornfully called *gicgoc*.

The Northmen left as great a mark on Ireland as they did on England. For one thing, they founded almost every important city in the land, including Dublin, Waterford, and Limerick which had all begun as viking camps.

They also taught the Irish the necessity of forgetting tribal feuds and at least occasionally establishing some sort of Irish unity. It was because of this lesson that Brian Boru, the famous king of Munster, was able, in 1002, to rule all of Ireland, and finally, in 1014, to defeat the invaders at the battle of Clontarf just outside of Dublin. Although the white-haired Brian was slain in his tent after this battle, Norse power in Ireland was broken forever.

Finally, the Northmen brought wealth to Erin. Some of it came from honest trade, but much of it was viking booty which had been amassed in world-wide raids and carried to Ireland for safety.

When, indeed, the Irish took Limerick, which was a viking capital, they were amazed at all the splendor they found. Besides silver and gold, there were beautiful leather saddles (probably Moorish leather saddles brought from Spain); woven fabrics of every kind and color; and beautiful and variegated silk and satin raiment.

"It is both scarlet and green, all in one weaving!" cried the bedazzled Irish bog dwellers who were used to drab homespun.

In this age of high adventure and of thrusting out in every direction, the men from Denmark and Norway also launched attacks against Frisland (Frisia, or Holland), Frankland, and Valland (France south of Brittany). All these had once been ancient Gaul.

Here they found conditions more like those in Britain than in Ireland.

Gaul had been an opulent Roman province. It, too, had had luxurious villas, arched aqueducts, temples, amphitheaters, and baths. It had a rich agriculture. Its artisans produced the famous *terra sigillata* pottery—red clay with glazed relief—as well as handsome glass and bronzeware. And up and down its roads and its already well-established inland waterways there moved a heavy traffic which would not be equaled until modern times.

Then, as the Roman Empire fell apart, it too was attacked by Teutonic tribesmen. Almost at the same time that the Angles, Saxons, and Jutes were crossing the North Sea to England, the Salian (salt-water) and the Riparian (riverbank) Franks were moving across the Rhine.

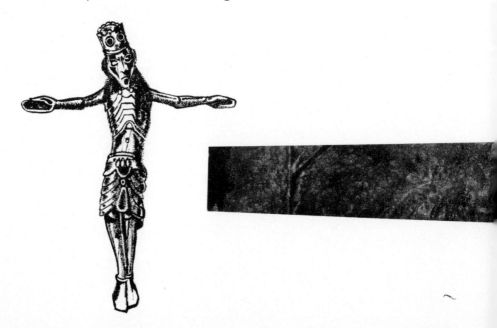

They, too, destroyed and plundered. And then, under their first rulers, the so-called Merovingians—descendants of the semi-legendary King Merovaeus—they built their own Frankish civilization.

But there was an important difference. The Franks had a land boundary with the men from the north; it was the Eider River in modern Schleswig. Consequently, their first contacts with sea raiders were on dry land.

These contacts began soon after the Franks had established themselves in their new lands, and as early as 700, a Dutch missionary, St. Willibrord, left his see at Utrecht to preach Christianity to the pagan Danes who now lived between the Baltic and the North Sea. Nothing came of it. For one reason, do-nothing Childeric was king of the Franks. But in 768 Charlemagne mounted the throne and six years later he marched to the banks of the Elbe. The Danes now became truly alarmed. Sigefridus, their king, did nothing, but was succeeded by his son Godfred, who decided to strike back.

He ordered his country's frontiers to be fortified with an earth rampart which he called the Danevirke (Dane's work).

"Build it," he commanded, "from the East Salt Water"— that is, the Baltic—"to the Western Ocean. It must protect the whole North bank of the Eider River, and shall have only one gate wide enough for wagons and riders."

He also secured his flank by attacking the Slavic Obritites (allies of Charlemagne) and destroying their capital on the shores of the Baltic near present-day Rostock.

After that, in 810, he invaded Charlemagne's own realm with a fleet of two hundred vessels, won three battles, and demanded and received one hundred pounds of silver from Charlemagne's lieutenant.

But not until Charlemagne had died and had been followed

by his son, Louis the Pious, and by his quarreling grandsons, did the Danes dare go farther.

Then the men from the flat islands and the narrow belts poured into the Frankish kingdom as they had into "Engle-land" and Ireland.

They occupied the sand-dune island of Walcheren at the mouth of the Meuse. They sacked Quentovic, now sanded up, but then an important seaport on the English Channel. They sailed around the rocky tip of Brittany to attack Noir-moutier and the Île de Ré.

As the monks of the former fled to the salt marshes over and over again with the possessions they could save, they added a new line to be chanted in church.

*"A furore Normanorum libera nos domine!"* From the fury of the Northmen, deliver us, O Lord!

These Northmen—or other Northmen—also assaulted Rouen, and their ships sailed up the Seine to Paris. Rouen, along with Quentovic and Dorstadt, was an important city of Frankland, but Paris was still only a small town of wooden houses and muddy streets on the Île de la Cité, the little island in the middle of the modern city where the Cathedral of Notre Dame now stands.

But it was strategically important, and so the sea raiders besieged it not once but many times; and once they besieged it both by land and by sea. This was in 885 when another King Sigefridus encamped before it with a host of forty thousand men and seven hundred ships. He lingered in front of Paris for two years, but although its bridges went up in flames, the city did not fall.

Nantes was attacked too, on the day of the feast of St. John the Baptist when it was crowded with celebrants.

This was one of the most savage attacks of all. Not content

with slaughtering Christians in the streets, the marauders burst into the church and cut down the bishop as he knelt before the altar. Then they sailed off, their sixty-seven ships laden with what they had taken.

"They seize Bordeaux, Périgueux, Limoges, Angoulème, and Toulouse!" cried an unhappy Frenchman. "Angers, Tours, and Orléans are annihilated! Chartres is occupied! Evereux and Bayeux are plundered!"

Most of these attacks were by Danes. But, soon, Norwegians joined the ravagers.

And finally Rollo appeared. Rollo was Hrolf Ganger, or Rolf the Walker, called this because he was so huge of body that no little Norwegian pony could carry him; he had to go on foot.

A turbulent man who had been banished from Norway for raiding cattle belonging to King Harald Fairhair's subjects, Rollo decided to become a Christian when he got to France and to swear allegiance to the French king, Charles the Simple.

To be sure, he did this in his own rough viking way. Told that he must pay homage by kneeling down and kissing the king's foot, he refused firmly and with many an oath. Then he ordered one of his men to do it for him. The latter obeyed, but instead of bending down, he seized Charles's foot and lifted it to his lips. Charles fell over backward as the vikings roared with laughter.

Nevertheless—this was in 911—he then and there made Rollo the first Duke of Normandy.

Rollo's followers became the Normans. They soon were speaking French instead of Norwegian and they intermarried with the people they had conquered to produce the Northman French race that would conquer England in 1066. But they still kept most of their Northman characteristics.

In the east Swedish vikings moved outward too. They moved down the great rivers of Russia to the Baltic and even farther, a slow progress compared to the raids upon the west, but it carried them over great distances and to even richer lands.

It began far, far earlier than the western raids. Longer ago than we can say, tribesmen from Swedish Uppland and East Gautland (north and south of present-day Stockholm) had been slowly penetrating western Finland. There many of them mingled with the native Asiatic Finno-Ugrians—like the Turks and Hungarians, these came from the distant Altai Mountains—giving them the blond appearance that many of them have today. Then they pushed on to Lake Ladoga where they founded, or took over, the fortified town of Staraja Ladoga not more than eight miles from the lake's shores. There they established themselves as traders and rulers. They even adopted Finnish and Slavic languages and customs whenever it was necessary.

From there they moved slowly southward.

"I met," wrote an Arab traveler around 850, "a sort of European who brought beaver skins and black fox furs and swords from the furthest part of their land down to the Black Sea. The Greek [Byzantine] Emperor charges a tithe upon their goods, and if they come down the Don, the prince of the Khazars"—a Turkic tribe most of which had adopted the Jewish faith—"takes his tithe also."

But many of them went down the Volga, passing through the market town of Bulgar on its great bend.

"Then they reach the Caspian and take ship again. Sometimes they bring their wares as far as Baghdad where Slavic eunuchs interpret for them."

Try to picture them as they rode into the latter city upon their bad-tempered "ships of the desert." These lurched almost as crazily as did one of their swift vessels when buffeted by a winter gale. Baghdad was then the most fabulous place in the world. Its white houses gleamed in the hot sun. Its palaces were beautifully tiled or decorated with marble or with alabaster filigree. The veiled woman whom you passed on the street might be a daughter of the caliph in disguise. The man at the street corner might be Sinbad the Sailor.

But Baghdad was also one of the world's greatest marts, and as the rough blond-bearded men of the north rode into it, not forgetting to look to their swords, they knew that the bales they brought with them carried the best things that their seas and forests produced.

What would they buy with them?

The Varangians—for that is what the vikings were called in eastern Europe—also set up Northman rule in Novgorod. Indeed, Rurik, a Scandinavian, actually founded the dynasty that ruled Russia until the days of the Romanovs. The Varangians attacked Micklegarth (Constantinople) at least three times—in 860, 941, and 944—and finally forced the Byzantine emperor to sign a treaty with them.

In 912, according to an Arab writer, they assembled a fleet of five hundred vessels on the Caspian; took Baku, which even then was noted for its petroleum; and marched inland to Azerbaijan. They plundered as they went.

The vikings made forays into the Mediterranean too, and one of these was particularly daring.

In 859, two chieftains, Hasteinn and Bjorn Ironside, another son of Ragnar Hairybreeches, left the Garonne River with a fleet of sixty-two vessels. They first attacked northwestern Spain. The Prince of Navarre paid them a ransom of ninety thousand gold denarii, but in Asturias, the Emir of Seville, shouting "May Allah curse them!," drove them off with something resembling Greek fire. Next they attacked Lisbon, but were driven off again.

Then, as rainbow-tinted dolphins arched around their prows, the fleet sailed through the Strait of Gibraltar to land in Morocco, where they captured a substantial amount of "blue men"—their name for Negroes—whom they sent back to Dublin to be sold as slaves.

After that, they raided the Balearic Islands; landed in southern France; marched overland to Arles; and spent the winter in the flat marshy delta country of the Camargue. In the spring they struggled more than one hundred miles up the swift Rhone currents to Valence.

Then they turned south to Italy. There they sacked the tiny fishing seaport of Luna on the Gulf of Spezia a little south of Genoa. A French chronicler tells the story:

The vikings, he said, had been told that Rome was in Italy, and when they saw little Luna, they thought it was mighty Rome. But Rome was too great to be taken except by trickery, and so they tried a trick.

Marching up to Luna's walls, they shouted that their chieftain, Hasteinn, was dead, and asked permission to bring the old heathen's body into the city to give him a Christian burial.

"By the Pope!" they cried. "Or by some Bishop!"

"Bring him in," said the men of Luna.

But when the vikings were in the city, Hasteinn leaped from his bier and slew the brocaded churchmen who had just read the first words of the service. Then his followers seized weapons hidden in their garments.

"Rome" fell to them in a matter of minutes, but when they found that this was not really Rome, they flew into a wild frenzy and destroyed the little city.

Next, they proceeded south again, burning Pisa as they went and attacking many other Italian seacoast cities.

Finally, they reached Serkland (Saracen Africa), including Egypt and Palestine. On the way they had raided some of the Greek islands. They cruised in the Aegean and perhaps the Sea of Marmora. Some of them may even have seen the "metal"—that is, the shining golden—towers of imperial Byzantium (Constantinople) just as their cousins, the Varangians, were approaching across the Black Sea.

It was not until 862 that the adventurers turned homeward, reaching the Garonne once more, some of them continuing to Ireland. Only twenty-two of the original sixty-two ships were left, but even at that the voyage was considered a success. "A king should seek honor, not a long life," was one of their sayings.

The *Hávamál* ("The Sayings of the High One"—that is, one-eyed Odin) expresses the same sentiments. The *Hávamál* is an ancient Northman poem filled with wise lore and pithy sayings.

"Cattle die," says the *Hávamál*, "and kinsmen die, and you yourself will die one day. But fame—fair fame—will never die."

They had found fame—and whole shiploads of booty too.

But Hasteinn and Bjorn were not the only Northmen to win renown and fortune in the deep-blue inland sea.

Harald Hardraade (Harold the Hardruler, who was king of Norway from 1046 to 1066) was one of the most valiant and the most able of all Northman kings. First with his brother Magnus, then as sole ruler, he governed Norway with an iron hand and brought the land to order. He also tried to conquer England—and he died there. Two weeks before William the Conqueror landed near Hastings, he himself came ashore in the north. He marched southward with English King Harold's brother, but near Stamford Bridge he was struck in the throat by an arrow; thus the course of English history was changed.

But long before that, this huge man—he was seven feet tall—with golden hair and with one eyebrow higher than the other, had been an adventurer in the Byzantine east. He had served the empress Zoe, amassing enough gold to be the richest man in the north; fought the Arabs in Sicily; taken eight castles in the Holy Land; and, it is said, helped the empress blind her husband.

But he was as capable of using his wits as well as his sword. When he sought to leave Zoe's employ, she imprisoned him. He was set free by a noble lady. Then he and his men stole two ships and rowed toward the Bosporus. There was an iron chain across the harbor mouth.

"Row to it," he commanded. They reached it. "Now come aft!"

Up into the air went the ship's bow and they were halfway over.

"Now go forward!" The stern went up. They crossed the barrier.

When he was next heard of, he was in Russia where he married the daughter of King Jarolsav.

Sigurd the Jerusalemfarer was another Northman who fared well in the Mediterranean.

Sigurd was a son of King Magnus Barelegs (so called because he had learned to wear kilts when he was marauding in Scotland), and with his brothers Olaf and Eystein he mounted the Norwegian throne in 1103. Just then men came back from the Holy Land "with many novelties to talk about"—the Northmen loved strange tales—and with many boasts about the wealth that could be won.

Sigurd decided to try crusading himself.

Leaving Eystein and young Olaf behind, "to rule upon their joint account," Sigurd went to England where William the Conquerer now reigned, and then on by way of Galicia, southern Spain, and the Balearic Islands to Sicily, Cyprus, Acre, Jerusalem, and finally to Constantinople.

"It is told," says a saga, "that he had his horse shod with golden shoes before he rode into the city, and managed that one should come off in the street, but that none of his men should notice it."

Let the Byzantines scramble for it! It was tinsel to a haughty viking.

During this crusade of his, Sigurd also rendered an important service to a ruler who had viking ancestors.

You will recall that Rollo swore allegiance to the Frankish king and was given Normandy as a reward. But although his people were now half Frenchmen, the restless Northman blood still flowed in their veins, and this, around 1030, led Norman barons and their soldiers to invade southern Italy and then Sicily where they drove out the Saracens and set up a domain of their own.

But although Sicily's ruler at the time, Roger II, was as powerful as many monarchs, he took no title higher than duke. Sigurd, filled with Northman pride, decided to do something about that.

"King Sigurd"—says a saga—"came to Sicily and remained there a long time. He was splendidly entertained. Every day Duke Roger stood at the company's table, doing service to the king. But on the seventh day as this happened, King Sigurd took the duke by the hand, led him up to the high seat, and saluted him as king. 'I give you the right,' he said, 'to rule forever under this title.'"

In the days of old, a king had the power to make another man king.

From King Roger II descended a line whose enlightenment has rarely been surpassed. In Palermo, with its rustling palm trees and its golden oranges and lemons, they built splendid palaces and magnificent churches. These were brilliant with tiles and decorated with mosaics. One of the most famous of the descendants of Roger was Frederick II, who also took the title of Roman emperor. He was the patron of the earliest writers of Italian poetry, writing some fine poetry himself as well as a book on falconry which was the first scientific bird book ever written, and his court drew learned men from the whole western world.

But less than three centuries earlier, his forebears had been viking plunderers who ravaged with fire and with sword.

# To Iceland and to
# Vinland the Good

As they surged outward from their homeland, these seafarers and sea-fighters went to many other places too.

In the Baltic, for example, they fought with the Wends of Wendland, a Slavic people who dwelt in northern Germany, and with the tribesmen of Samland near the mouth of the Vistula; and with the Letts and the Lithuanians; and with the rude and backward Estonian pirates of Estland (East Land) who lived on the far shores of the Gulf of Riga near modern Leningrad.

They even attacked their fellow vikings at Jömsberg, a strategic fortress and place of refuge on the south shore of the Baltic near the mouth of the Oder River. The Jömsberg vikings were an almost monastic order of warriors who allowed no woman within their stronghold and who were sworn to blood brotherhood. This order was supposedly founded by

King Harald Bluetooth of Denmark (940–986) as a bulwark against Wendland. But soon the Jömsberg warriors were as dangerous as the Wends, and in 1043 young King Magnus the Good found it necessary to storm their robber's den and burn every building to the ground.

In the British Isles the Northmen revisited the Hebrides and set up a Norse earldom there.

They landed in the Shetland Islands and made it a Norwegian colony, having brought with them the kind of shaggy little Norse ponies which had not been able to carry Rollo. Shetland ponies are now world famous, and a majority of present-day Shetlanders are of Norwegian descent.

Their ships came to the Orkneys and there, too, a Northman was made *jarl,* or earl. These *jarls* heavily taxed the islanders, but also showed them a better way of living. For instance, they showed the native Picts and Scots a way of keeping warm and of cooking their food which they still use today. Finding no firewood on the islands, one of the Northmen, Einar, sailed to the Scottish mainland, and had his men dig peat there. He brought it back again, and from then on was called Turf Einar.

They invaded Scotland. Although Shakespeare's play does not say this, it was actually a "Norwegian," Thorfinn the Red, who helped Macbeth to power. The vikings left their mark on Scotland. Galloway received its name from the Gall-Gaidhells (the Irish Norse) who invaded from Ireland, while such Scots-sounding names as Macauley, McIvar, McSwann, and even Lamont come from the Norse. They come from Olaf, Ingvar, Svein, and from *logman,* which means "lawman."

More distantly, Northmen from Denmark drove their ships to the Faeroe Islands far out in the Atlantic Ocean. They hunted sea-bird eggs and landed sheep there. The Faeroes are still Danish, and sheep still crop the sparse grass, but the principal industry is now fishing.

During the Viking Age, the Northmen also sailed up to and around the North Cape.

Almost seven hundred years before Sir Richard Chancellor journeyed from London to Archangel on the White Sea in 1553 and thus "opened up" a trade route to northern Russia, a viking explorer had made the same journey.

He was Ottar, a powerful chieftain who ruled in the northernmost part of Norway. Ottar was a rich man for that part of the world, owning twenty cows, thirty sheep, twenty pigs, and six hundred reindeer. But he was not wealthy enough to suit himself, so he entered the service of Alfred the Great of England.

Alfred ordered him to sail northward as far as he could and then to turn eastward. This he did, but he found the voyage disappointing.

"The White Sea whales are small," Ottar reported. "They are only twenty-seven feet long. Off western Norway, they are sixty feet long."

But he continued to the north Russian coast where he found natives who were glad to do business with him. They were Finns or Lapps who sold him ermine and the finest walrus ivory he had ever seen.

He took a sample of it to the astonished King Alfred and thus introduced western Europe to the wonders of the north.

The Northmen made other voyages into or near the polar ice. In 1194, for example, they discovered Spitsbergen (present-day Svalbard), probably having discovered Novaya Zemlya even earlier.

Spitsbergen, with its tall and pointed mountain peaks, is a

bleak island covered with glaciers, lying almost due north of Norway and deep within the Arctic Circle. On the average, the Northern Lights, with their flickering blue, green, violet, and yellow, dance above it for 243 days of the year. Ice-bound for many months, the only birds and animals living on it permanently are the ptarmigan and the snowy owl, the walrus, the polar bear, the reindeer, and the fox.

Although not so far north as Spitsbergen, Novaya Zemlya is even colder. Sometimes the temperature drops to 58 degrees below zero.

Yet somehow the Northmen, their beards and mustaches frosted in the cold, managed to get to both of these places. Neither was revisited for at least four hundred years.

But not even Europe and not even the European Arctic was big enough for the adventuring Northmen.

Companioned only by the stinging and salty spume, the gray-winged sea gull, and the brave little stormy petrel, it was not long before they were sailing outward and onward toward the world's fabled edge. Beyond this, it was thought, lurked only kraken and other legendary sea monsters of northern seas.

Yet even when the gales howled, they were not down-hearted. Indeed their skalds, or poets, made songs about their fury and sang them even louder than the weather.

> The sea begins to swell.
> The clouds press down.
> Witchcraft
> Sets the ocean to boiling.
>
> We cannot see the waves
> We have come so far to the west.
> The sea glows

As if one saw embers.
The breakers fall all over themselves.
Then those swan-tops lift to the sky.

Often the vessel and those aboard it were saved only by frantic bailing. All bailed just as everyone toiled at the oar. When they were on the high seas, chieftain and followers and even thralls were equals. Only the helmsman was ever a specialist, for it was not everyone who could pick the course unerringly or manage the heavy steering oar which was always on the right hand or starboard (*steer board*) side.

Saxo Grammaticus, the famous medieval Danish historian, tells us about the first place these ocean-faring Northmen came to.

"To the west of Norway," he wrote, "lies a great island with the mighty ocean all around it. It is miserable to live in but it is filled with marvels. On it there is a spring whose waters are so evil that no man can bear their stench. Its vapor burns everything that comes near it into the hardness of stone. Other springs suddenly fill with gushing water and then blow a mass of spray upward. Then the bubbling stops and their waters hide deep underground.

"On the island, too, is a mountain so wreathed in never-ending fire that it looks like glowing rock. Belching forth huge flames, it keeps its crest in an eternal blaze.

"Hither, also, at fixed and appointed seasons, there drifts a boundless mass of ice and when it begins to dash against the rugged reefs, there is heard from the deep a roaring of voices and a din and clamor so loud and so unearthly that it is supposed to come from those doomed to everlasting torture by the iniquity of their sins."

After Saxo had written this (around 1200), he scratched his beard in puzzlement.

"How," he asked, "can a land lying so close to the extremest cold find the abundant fuel to keep up these undying fires?"

Saxo was talking about Iceland, the northernmost point of whose 40,000 square miles just touches the Arctic Circle. He was describing Great Geysir which has given its name to every geyser in the world. He was witnessing an eruption of one of the many volcanoes there like Oerafajökull, the loftiest mountain, or Hekla, which is still sputtering. He was painting a picture of the glittering armada of huge icebergs which in those days choked the northern fjords.

There are several versions of how and when Iceland was discovered by the Northmen. According to one of them, a viking named Nadd-Odd left the Faeroes in 861 for his home in Norway. He was blown off his course and came to "a large mountainous land" in the western ocean. He climbed the highest peak he could find and then sailed away in a blinding snowstorm. He called the land Snowland; it was named Iceland by Raven Floki, another Norwegian, who was the first man to see the endless ice fields described by Saxo.

Nadd-Odd was followed by Gardar, a Swede. Gardar, too, was blown off his course. But it is more likely that the Norse expeditions to Iceland were carefully planned. For whether or not the island had been discovered by the Romans— Roman coins have been found there—or even by Pytheas, a Greek from Marseilles who traveled the whole north in 325 B.C. and who spoke of "an island called Thule six days northward from Britain," it was certainly known in Ireland.

The famous St. Brendan (484–577) is said to have come to a steep and rocky land on which there was "a great hellish mountain which appeared full of clouds and smoke about its summit." Brendan was an Irish saint who sailed the open ocean in a flimsy boat, and there is even a legend that he reached Florida or the West Indies. But he *did* reach Iceland and he left his monks behind him.

"There we found Christian men," said the first Northman to settle there, "but they went away because they would not live with heathens. They left behind them Irish books and croziers and bells."

The Northmen called these Irish Christians *papar,* or "Pope's men."

The early history of Iceland is related in an old volume, the *Landnámabók,* or "Book of the Land Takers." This tells that in the two generations after 875—when the first permanent settlers arrived—three thousand families emigrated there. It was almost like the coming of the Pilgrims to New England.

Like the Pilgrims, too, these Northmen came to preserve their old freedom and to escape tyrannical rule.

"Owing to Harald Fairhair's oppression," says a saga, "many people fled from the country, and many uninhabited lands were settled. At that time Iceland was discovered."

Harald Fairhair was the great king who united Norway around 900. But if many Norwegian vikings sailed into the west to escape Harald's hard hand, almost certainly they learned there was a land to sail to in St. Brendan's native land, and it is equally certain that many an Irishman came with them.

Aud the Deep-Minded came to the island as a widow. No longer a queen, she was, however, a great lady with wide domains. She brought with her many Irish slaves (the Northmen called them thralls), one of whom, Erp, founded an important Icelandic family.

Helgi the Lean, who was the richest of the early settlers had an Irish mother, and Olaf Pá (Olaf Peacock), who was famous for his gaudy clothes, was also partly Irish.

Even Njal, considered to be the wisest man in Iceland, and hero of the famous *Njal's Saga,* has a name of Celtic origin. It is another form of Neil.

From Iceland the Northmen went still farther exactly one hundred years later. They went on to Greenland, which is not surprising. What is surprising is that they waited so long. For Greenland is not even two hundred miles from Iceland, and the mountains of the two countries are so lofty that halfway across the water separating them one can see the mountain peaks of both.

Furthermore, Northmen had already come very close to

Greenland. Late in the ninth century, one Gunnbjorn, son of
Ulf the Crow, had, like the vikings who first sighted Iceland,
been driven by storm winds westward until he had come to
a group of small rocks just off the Greenland coast. He called
them Gunnbjornarsker, or Gunnbjorn's skerries.

But it was only when Eric the Red had been outlawed
from both Norway and Iceland for manslaughter that a
serious attempt to reach Greenland was made.

Told that he must leave the island, red-haired Eric made
ready a ship and set to sea. Some of his friends followed him
to say farewell, thinking that he was going back to Norway.
But as he cleared the headland, he turned in another direction.

"I am off to Gunnbjorn's skerries!" he called out to them.
Then he disappeared into the graying dusk.

Half a year later, he returned. He had reached the shiver-
ing and ice-laden east coast of a new land; had rounded its
dangerous southernmost point; had turned northward up the
milder west coast; wintered on bleak Ericksey (Eric's Island),
and then sailed northward until he was blocked by ice.

But as he did this he noted, at the head of a deep fjord, a
narrow strip of relatively fertile ground. Under the beetling
and bare cliffs, there were Arctic wildflowers. He decided to
settle there.

"I have just found a wonderful new place," he told people
upon returning to Iceland. "It's name is Greenland."

Later he admitted why he had given it such a name.

"If I gave it a fine name," he explained, "men will long to
go there."

Evidently the ruse worked, for when he returned a year
later, twenty-five ships accompanied him. Fourteen arrived
safely, and the men and women aboard them went ashore.
Eric, they discovered, had already chosen the best spot for his

GREENLAND

ICELAND

FAEROE IS.

NORTH AMERICA

SHETLAND IS.

HEBRIDES IS.

ORKNEY IS.

North Sea

NEWFOUNDLAND

Dublin

York

DENM

Limerick

London

Waterford

Atlantic Ocean

Quentor

Rouen

Paris

Noirmoutier

CALIPHATE OF CORDOVA

Ro

AFRICA

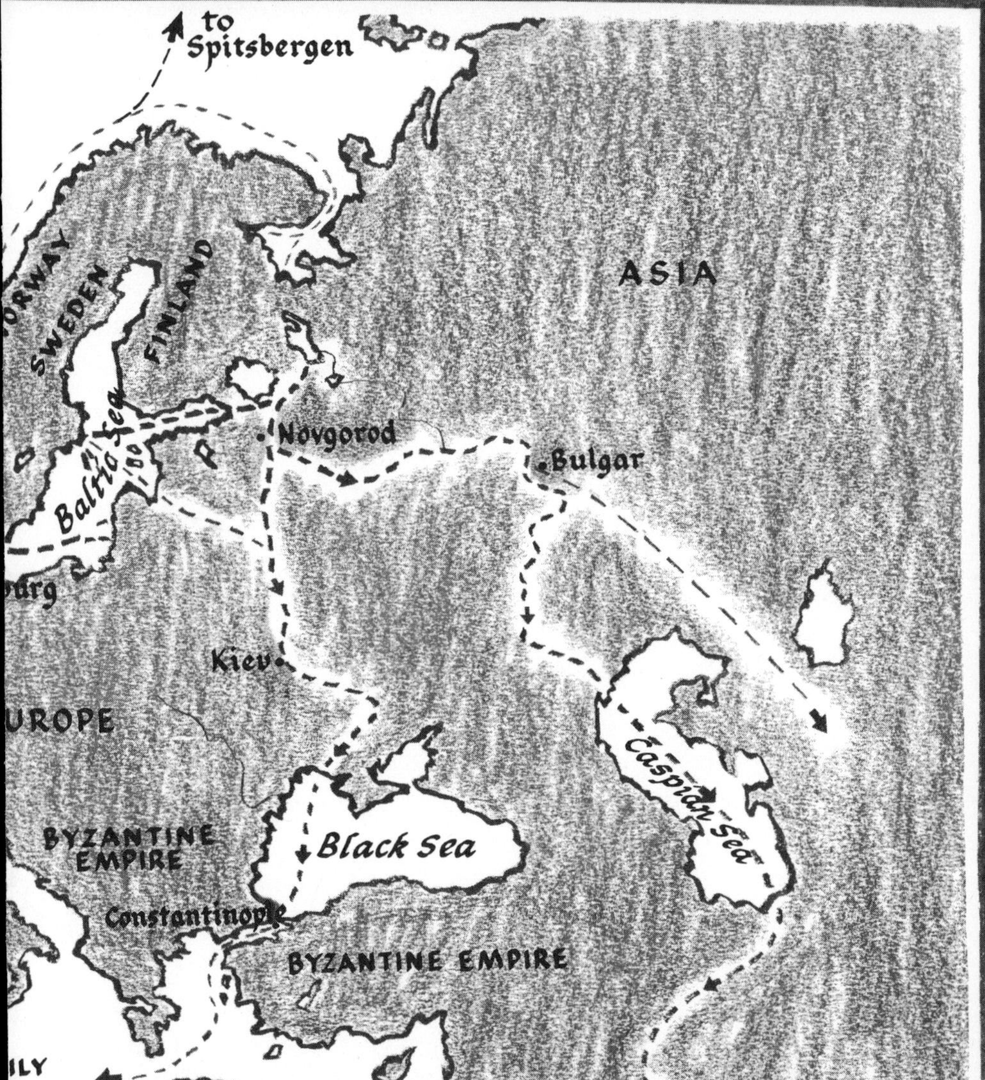

to
Spitsbergen

NORWAY

SWEDEN

FINLAND

Baltic Sea

Novgorod

Bulgar

burg

Kiev

EUROPE

Caspian Sea

BYZANTINE
EMPIRE

Black Sea

Constantinople

BYZANTINE EMPIRE

ASIA

ILY

Mediterranean Sea

Baghdad

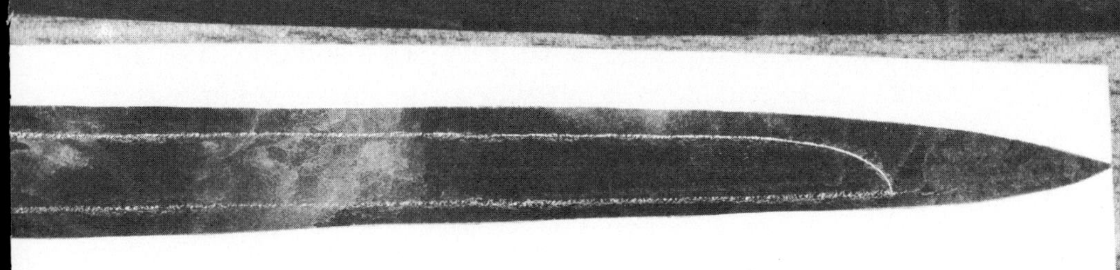

farm, Brattahlid, or Steep Slope, but there was other land available, and soon near present-day Julianehaab the first settlement arose. Ten years later and at least two hundred miles farther north they built a second settlement.

In these two places and in widely scattered hamlets in between, these settlers and their descendants lived for nearly five hundred years. They built stone churches—for not long after 1000 most Northmen had become Christian—and long stone houses roofed with turf, and they wrested a precarious living in the inhospitable clime. In the short Arctic summer they tried to grow grain, and they certainly raised cattle, sheep, goats, and swine. There are signs of a native iron-working industry, but the iron must have been imported. They lived on whale, seal, fish, bear, and reindeer, and they exported polar bear skins, walrus tusk, and perhaps narwhal ivory, and the famous Greenland falcons.

Then suddenly the Northmen disappeared. Some people think that they died of malnutrition or of smallpox, but more believe that they were slain by the advancing Eskimos.

But not even Greenland's icy mountains were the viking's farthest venture to the west. Beyond them lay North America, extending from the tundras of Baffin Island to distant Panama.

This land, too, the vikings discovered by accident.

In 985, a Norwegian, Bjarni Herjulfson, set sail from Norway in his sturdy *hafskip,* an ocean-going vessel with broader beam and higher freeboard than the viking warship, to seek his father Herjulf who had settled in Iceland. But by the time Bjarni reached Iceland, his father had gone on to Greenland with Eric.

Bjarni decided to follow them. He sailed on, and all went well until some three days later. Then suddenly the fair winds ceased as new gales blew in a freezing fog. For many days they could see neither sun nor stars and sometimes neither the ship's prow nor their hands held in front of them.

Then, just as it had come, the fog lifted and there was land ahead of them.

"Greenland!" the men shouted.

"It is not Greenland," said Bjarni, "for there are no mountains and it is forest-clad." Actually, although he did not know it, it was North America.

They turned northeast, and two days later made another landfall. But the shore was wooded here too.

"Still not Greenland!" cried Bjarni.

Three days later they saw land for a third time, and although it was rocky and inhospitable, Bjarni once again insisted that it was not the place he was looking for.

"There are still no glaciers," he pointed out, "and there are said to be enormous glaciers in Greenland."

On once more, and then land for the fourth time. They sped toward it on a southwest gale.

As they approached, they saw a ship moored off a headland and Bjarni steered toward it. On the shore, a man was walking and with his keen vision, Bjarni recognized his father. At last, they had reached Greenland.

But before he dropped anchor in Greenland Bjarni had discovered the New World. Five hundred years before Columbus he had seen the American continent and had come back and told about it. He was the first European known to have done so.

Fourteen years later, fellow Northmen actually landed in this new land and even tried to settle there.

Bjarni returned to Norway, much criticized for his lack of curiosity, and when Eric the Red's son Leif—who was then living with his father in Greenland—heard about it, he decided that he would find Bjarni's lands, and that, unlike his fellow Norwegian, he would go ashore on them.

He bought Bjarni's ship and persuaded him to divulge the courses he had sailed. Then Leif got together a crew of thirty-five men. In 999, they set out.

They came to Bjarni's land of rocks which Leif named Helluland (Flat Rock Land). It was probably Newfoundland.

Then they went on to Bjarni's lands of woods and beaches which Leif called Markland (Forest Land). This may have been Nova Scotia.

Finally, running before a northeast wind, they came to an island lying on the north side of the mainland and they landed to wait for good weather.

"There was dew on the grass, and putting it to our mouths, we thought that we had never tasted anything sweeter," they reported.

Then they came to a river which flowed out of a lake. There they cast anchor and put things in order for wintering. They built a large house, and to fill their larder, they fished for salmon and noted that they were larger than any they had ever seen before. They also noted that there was no frost (that must have been an exaggeration, but certainly it was warmer than the lands from which they came) and also that the days were much more equal in length. When the house was built Leif sent out exploring parties, and one day, one of the crew who was probably a south European came reeling back, rolling his eyes and pretending that he had had too much to drink.

"Good news!" he shouted. "I went no further than the others did, but I found something new. Vines and grapes grow here."

"Are you sure?" asked Leif.

"Certainly, for I was born in a country where there are plenty of both of them."

Leif thereupon named the country Vinland or "Vineland." Later it became known as Vinland the Good.

People are still arguing as to just where it was. A recently discovered map which dates back before Columbus' time only shows it as an island southwest of Greenland. But the ruins of a viking edifice have been discovered in northern Newfoundland and this may have been Lief's house. But it is more probable that it was somewhere between Boston and Chesapeake Bay.

Leif's expedition was followed by at least four others. These later vikings discovered a body of water with such swift currents that they called it Straumfjord or Stream Fjord. (Some people think this was Hell Gate near New York City.) They built booths around Leif's house, making a little village. They encountered American Indians, whom they called skraellings, and brought back tales of how the latter ran when a viking bull bellowed and of trading bits of red cloth and milk or butter for valuable furs. They also spoke of the skraellings' skin canoes and of an Indian weapon which consisted of a stave with a stone-filled pig's stomach at the end of it. The Algonquins had such a weapon!

In the end, the vikings fought the skraellings, and one of Leif's brothers, Thorvald, was slain by an Indian arrow. He was buried at a place which the vikings called Crossness. Another chieftain, Thorfinn Karlsefni, fathered a son in Vinland. The baby was named Snorri, and he, rather than Virginia Dare or Peregrine White, was the first white child born in this country.

There is even a chance that four hundred years later Northmen not merely landed on the Atlantic seacoast but penetrated as far inland as Minnesota. In 1898 a stone was discovered there with an inscription in runic letters which states that twenty-two Norwegians and eight Goths (Swedes) had come back from a fishing trip to their camp on a skerry in a lake to find that in their absence their companions had been slaughtered.

Many scholars say this is a forgery, like the skull of the famous Piltdown man which fooled anthropologists for nearly forty years, and this may well be so. Yet it is not impossible that Northmen did cross from Greenland to Hudson Bay and then up the rivers and the chains of lakes. It would not have been more daring or unlikely than many things we know they did.

# A Civilization in the North

But it would be wrong indeed to think that these men from the north, some of them dark and swarthy, but most with sun-bleached, tow-colored hair and ruddy complexions, were nothing but "ax-bearing barbarians" (the Byzantines' name for them) who appeared without warning over the horizon, and whose favorite pastime was burning cathedrals and chasing well-fed churchmen from their cloisters to murder them in cold blood.

It would be equally wrong to think of them as nothing but reckless adventurers who drove their craft wildly across the restless foaming of the stormy ocean—in a never-ending quest for places no one had ever seen before and far beyond the known world's end.

Ravage indeed they did—or at least some of them did.

Among these were the younger sons, for example, of the large families who found their ancestral lands too small for their energies and ambitions. Since the Northman kings and many among the rich Northmen practiced polygamy right up until the time of Christianity, there were many large families.

Among them were the scions of second, or so-called "Danish" marriages, for a great many Danes and Swedes and Norwegians *and* Icelanders—especially Icelanders!—like sailors, before and since, had not merely a sweetheart but a wife in every port!

These "Danish" marriages were not recognized and the sons and daughters they produced could not share in the *odal* —land and property which could not be sold but which had to go to the lawful heirs—of their fathers.

Hence they had to seek their fortunes abroad.

Among them were the mighty regional chieftains, who ruled with almost royal power in their own lands and who did not wish to become dependents of the increasingly powerful king, even though this sometimes increased both their wealth and their domains.

Among them were the doughty warriors who feared that they might not be slain in battle, and hence would not go to Valhalla. Valhalla was the Norse heaven to which slain heroes were taken by helmeted and armor-wearing maidens, the Valkyrie. There they passed their time in warlike games or drinking mead and ale.

Often the slain hero was a berserker, one of those mad fighters who rushed into the fray oblivious of wounds and hacking in every direction. These got their name either because they fought without armor—i.e., in a *bare shirt*—or because they wore a shaggy bearskin. Authorities disagree.

"Peace lasted so long," exulted one of the latter, Egil Woolshirt, when King Haakon the Good split the war arrow, thus calling up his followers, "that I feared that I might die of old age upon a bed of straw."

Among them, too, were the horny-handed lovers of ships—

*vikingr mikill* actually means great seafarer—with a gaze like the sea eagle, whose greatest joy was to venture forth on "the old gray widow-maker" with its racing white-maned steeds (the crested billows) and whose pulses beat faster when the salt spray flew stinging into their cheeks and they could hear the wake hissing behind them.

The Northmen ranged the earth, too, from the caravan cities beyond the Volga to New England and perhaps to the very heart of the present United States. But even though they raided and ranged, spreading the fame and terror of the viking name throughout the four quarters of the globe, by far the greater part of them remained behind in Scandinavia.

(Some of them, of course, roved and stayed behind too. One of the sagas tells of a Shetland chieftain who sowed his crops in the spring; went "a-viking" while they grew and ripened; came home to harvest them; and then went "a-viking" again. He was by no means the only one.)

It was a hard and difficult land, particularly for the people of the olden days who did not have modern methods for dealing with the cold.

As the Byzantine historian Procopius reported fourteen centuries ago: "The sun at the summer solstice never sets there for forty days, but not more than six months later for another forty days it is not seen for the same length of time."

When it did reappear, messengers came racing down from a high mountain to report that they had seen its rim.

"Then a mighty festival is held. For although this happens every year, each year they fear that it may never become light again."

The snow drifted roof-high in the winter and the summers were brief and fickle. In much of the country there was little else but bare rocks, wild heath, and quaggy bogs.

But in this bitter climate, whose "general dreariness,"

according to an ancient writer, was such that no man "in his right mind" would leave the sunny south to visit it; in this hard and difficult land; on the narrow strips of fertile meadow between Norway's rugged mountains and wild fells and her blue fjords; along the shores of Sweden's many, beautiful lakes; on the glacier-deposited soil of Denmark, they did what their ancestors had been doing from time immemorial.

They farmed or hunted or fished. And quite often they did all three.

At least as early as Roman days, the larger, and more or less communal settlements had begun to break up in favor of homesteads. It is possible that this happened even before that. There is some reason to believe that the so-called *bönde* —or free farmer—system which pertained in Norway almost to modern times began at least by 500 B.C.

These first farms were close to the salt water. But soon the Northmen began to use the iron ax, which they wielded so

skillfully that they could not only rough-hew planks for houses and ships, but also clear away the primeval forest. They then began to climb to higher altitudes where the drainage was better and the frosts were shorter and less severe.

But even as it moved away from the shore, the well-organized *gaarde*—patriarchal or "grandfather" farm, called this because its proprietor was usually the oldest male in his family—was always placed where there was fishing nearby and where good hunting was available.

The reasons for this were obvious. Wheat and barley had been cultivated in Scandinavia since before 1500 B.C. Oats were introduced not more than a thousand years later, and rye a little after 500 B.C. There had been herds of swine and cattle and flocks of sheep and goats as long as can be remembered.

But although the long hours of summer daylight made some crops grow much faster than might have been expected and although fodder for the livestock was eked out by sending cattle and sheep to mountain summer farms with lush green pasture, not enough grain and fruit could always be raised to fill the larder or enough hay to feed the cattle.

The near-by rivers, however, teemed with salmon and trout, while the inlets and the offshore seas were filled with herring, cod, and mackerel, as well as whales, seals, and walruses. The Northmen hunted the larger sea mammals with bow and arrow just as was done in southwest Norway up to the last century. They fished for the smaller saltwater fish in the same seaworthy, double-ended craft that are used off the Lofoten Islands even today.

Elk and red deer stalked through the forest. There were bear. There were enormous herds of reindeer. Ducks, of course, blackened the waters of every pond, and the North-man who had a falcon or a trusty bow or crossbow could bag all he needed. And on "snow skates," or primitive skis, he could silently slip between the trees to snare grouse or ptarmigan. Thus, even if there was a bad year, he could live handsomely.

The Northmen who remained at home also became merchants and traders.

(As a matter of fact, so did some of those who ventured abroad. The vikings, says a man who has studied them, were as much traders as they were robbers. Often, indeed, they only became robbers when their trading ventures fared badly.)

They had been merchants, incidentally, almost as long as they had been farmers, or even fishermen or hunters.

Pytheas—the ancient Greek who *may* have discovered Ice-land—certainly did visit Scandinavia.

"There," he wrote, "I came to a people called the Gutones [the Goths] who live on an island which is called Abanus [perhaps Gotland]. On this island, amber is washed ashore and the inhabitants sell it to the Teutones."

The Northmen of the Viking Age still traded in amber, but other trade was more important.

Slaves, for example. Slavery played an important part in Norse life. Every important household had thralls (slaves) and often these held important positions such as steward or housekeeper. And although a woman who was a thrall had to dress plainly and a male thrall had to have his hair cropped and wear white wadmal (a coarse wool fabric), they were usually treated well. They could always buy their freedom.

Some thralls were the descendants of the aboriginal inhabi-tants, the dark people whom the blond Germanic tribesmen found when they came to Scandinavia. Others were captives taken in battle or raids, like the beautiful Melkorka who was sold to an Icelander and became the mother of the rich and famous Olaf Peacock.

But there was also a slave trade. The Northmen bought slaves and also sold them.

Furs, including mink and sables and fox, wolf, and bearskins.

Pottery, not only heavy clay vessels but delicately decorated cups and vases.

Iron axes, swords, scissors for shearing sheep, knives, arrowheads, needles, and similar objects.

(Thus, Scandinavian iron and steel, which is now so famous, put in a very early appearance.)

Silver brooches and other silver and gold jewelry.

Buckles, as well as pins and clasps, fashioned of bronze.

Being traders, and traders whose ventures extended from London to South Russia, Byzantium, and Baghdad, it did not take the Northmen long to build towns such as Björkö in Sweden, Sciringssalar in southwest Norway, and Hedeby in southern Denmark. Of these, as renowned as any was Hedeby, founded in the ninth century. It covered sixty acres and was protected by a semicircular earthwork. A stream divided it in two, and along this were the merchants' houses, which also served as their shops. Made of wattle and daub, each was enclosed by a fence of plaited hurdles.

An Arab writer says that Hedeby was large, dirty, and poor, and that its people lived on dried fish and that their singing sounded like the howling of dogs.

But Saxon merchants from Hamburg and Bremen, and even Byzantines, Frisians, and Franks thought better of it. According to them, one could visit the city without fear. Probably you could, for even while the Northmen were pirates and raiders, they attached great importance to good conduct on the part of their merchants.

This is well illustrated in the *Speculum regale,* or "Mirror for Kings," which was written in Norway in the Middle Ages to tell youthful Northmen how to conduct themselves either in the king's household or in the busy mart.

"To be a merchant," it says, "both knowledge and experience is necessary. The merchant must be courteous, pleasing in manners, generous, a good judge of values, honest and open. He should set a good table, dress well, and seek the company of the best people. He should study all laws too, but if a man wishes to be a merchant there is no law which he should study more carefully than the Barkeyjarretir (Björkö Island Law) or Law of Trade.

In addition to prospering on their farms and becoming wealthy through plundering and trade, the Northmen of the Viking Age developed a way of living characterized by "that relative progress in the arts, in science, and in statecraft" which is the essence of a civilization.

The Northman civilization was, incidentally, the most northerly one that had ever existed until that time.

For nearer to the Arctic Circle and beyond it were only the Scrithifini, or "Snowshoe Finns" (actually Lapps) who dwelt in a Stone Age culture near the ice-choked Arctic Ocean, living on reindeer, whale and walrus, clothing themselves in the skins of seal and polar bear, and since the Scrithifini bone-tipped spears and arrowheads were no match for viking swords, paying a tribute of ivory and walrus sinews to their mighty neighbors to the south.

This civilization had its own kind of government, and its own social customs. It had its own art and its own architecture. The hard climate of the northland forced it to develop its own clothing and wearing apparel. It had its own games and sports. The Northmen were sportsmen even during the Viking Age. It had its own ethics and standards.

It had its own religion. Or perhaps it would be more accurate to say that it preserved deep into the Christian era the ancient religion of the old-time Germans, for the Northmen did not completely give up their pagan faith until 1000 A.D. or later. Although the names of certain of the gods were different, this was the faith of the ancient Germans described by Tacitus.

The civilization of the Northmen also had its own literature. It had its own—very important—Northman law.

# The Life of the Karl
# and of the Jarl

It was the kind of civilization that you would expect to find among men who wrested their living from the stormy ocean aboard ships which smelled of tar, or from stony fields which had been cleared out of the forest, or from the pine-scented forests themselves.

Fundamentally, it was a democratic civilization.

"We have no lord, but all are equal!" Rollo had cried when emissaries of the French king asked to be taken to the leader of the invading vikings.

This does not mean, however, that there were no classes among the Northmen. On the contrary, there were very clearly defined classes.

We can see the social organization of the Northmen vividly portrayed in an ancient Norse poem, the *Rígsthula*.

In it, Ríg (actually the god, Heimdall) descends to Middle-garth, the world of men, and there makes a long journey.

As he wanders, he meets various people.

77

First he meets Ai (great-grandfather) and Edda (great-grandmother).

> Edda gave birth to a boy-child
> And she swathed the swarthy one in swaddling clothes.
> They called him Thrall when they name-fastened him.
> His hair was black and his eyes were dull.
> His nails were dirty and his knuckles were gnarled.
> His fingers were thick and his face ugly.

Thrall (serf) grew up and was married to Thír (servant girl). Their sons were little better.

> Hay-pitcher, one was called. Another Surly.
> Slugabed. Swayback. Fat paunch.
> Stumpshanks. Stableboy. Sallow Skin.
> They laid fences, manured the fields, fattened the swine,
> Herded the goats and grubbed for peat.

After meeting Thrall, Ríg took up his staff and journeyed on again.

> Came he to another house. The door was unlatched.
> He entered. On the floor was a fire.
> Husband and wife sat there, busy at their tasks.
> Husband shaped a weaver's beam out of wood.
> Wife plied the loom.

They were Afi and Amma—grandfather and grandmother. Amma had a son too.

> They called him Karl (freeman) and lapped him in linen.
> He was ruddy of hue. Piercing was his gaze.
> He tamed the oxen, and tempered the ploughshare,
> Timbered houses, made a barn for his hay,
> Fashioned carts, and followed the plough.

Karl was given a wife. Her name was Snoer (daughter-in-law).

> They lived happily and had children.
> Hal (man). Bönde (farmer). Hauld (landed proprietor).
> Husbandman. Landlord. Franklin. Cottager.
> Roundbeard. Squarebeard. Burly and Swain and Smith.

Again Rig went on.

> He saw a hall then. Its door faced southward.
> It was shut and barred. There was a knocker on the door.

It was the home of Father and Mother.

> Straightway he entered. The floor was strewn with rushes.
> Father sat at his bench, twining his bowstring.
> He shaped elmwood into a bow, and shafted arrows.
> Mother looked at her arms and tidied her dress.

Rig sat down beside her.

> Of bleached flax then, she took a broidered cloth.
> She spread it on the table, and on it set
> Wheaten bread and a silver trencher
> With flitches of bacon and a roasted fowl
> And a crock of wine and some golden cups.

Like Edda and Amma, Mother had a son.

> She wrapped him in silk and sprinkled him with water.
> She called him Jarl (Earl, or Lord).
> His hair was yellow and his cheeks were fair.
> His eyes were sharp as a serpent's eyes.

Jarl was married to Erna, the daughter of Hersir, or chieftain. They had many children, the youngest of whom was called Kon.

Kon and his brothers were the personification of the golden Northman ideal. These brothers swam, sometimes even with full armor on. They rode, often without saddle or bridle. They shook spears and fended with their shields. The brothers shot arrows. They even learned how to play "tables," or chess.

But Kon—and Kon alone—had certain other accomplishments.

Kon only could carve runes—the life runes and the birth runes,
The runes that dull sword blades and calm the ocean.
Kon only knew bird speech and how to quench fires.
He only could soothe sorrows and heal the sick mind.
In his arms, he had the strength of eight men.

Because of his accomplishments Kon became Konungr, the man who could do things. Later he was simply Konung (without the r) or King.

But if the classes—*thrall,* or slave; *karl,* or freeman; *jarl,* or nobleman; and *konung,* or king—were thus clearly defined, except for the thrall, the freed thrall, and the cottagers (the humblest class of freemen), there was no insurmountable gap between them, nothing that even faintly resembled caste.

The rich landlord, for example—or even the more prosperous of the freeborn *karls*—could be like a *jarl* or even a king upon his own domains, while his wife in her own house had almost royal authority. Subject only to her husband, she commanded all the household slaves and serving folk; and into her charge were put all the clothes and linen chests and the closets and storerooms filled with provender. As symbol of her powers, there always hung from her belt a bunch of jangling keys. Because of this, she was often known as the *hanginlukla,* or "dangling-key lady."

Similarly, the king himself was not ashamed to act like a

prosperous farmer. The stepfather of King Olaf the Thick (995–1030)—the famous St. Olaf who became the patron saint of Norway—was Sigurd Sow, a local king in the Ringerike region of southern Norway.

"He was a careful householder," it was said of Sigurd, "who kept his people closely to their work, and often went about himself to inspect his fields of grain, his meadow lands, and his cattle."

He was on such an errand when his wife Aasta, Olaf's mother by a former marriage, sent word that her son was on his way. He was just about to proclaim himself king of all Norway.

The messenger found Sigurd bending over a plough.

"He had on a blue kirtle and blue hose, shoes which laced about the legs, a gray cloak [gray was the farmer's color], a gray wide-brimmed hat, a veil before his eyes [to keep away flies and mosquitoes], and a staff with a jet-silver head."

All he did was to change his clothes. Boots of cordovan instead of country shoes! A scarlet cloak instead of his gray one! Golden spurs and a golden helmet!

In the meanwhile Queen Aasta made her own preparations.

"She ordered four girls to bring out her decorations and hangings. Two housemen brought in straw for the floor; two others brought four-cornered tables and drinking jugs; two carried in victuals and placed the meat on the table; two were sent away to borrow in haste whatever was needed; and two struggled with the kegs of ale."

She was a housewife as much as her husband was a farmer.

And when the "fat fellow" (Olaf's enemies called him by this nickname) arrived with one hundred well-equipped retainers, he did not receive much more attention than any other visitor. People did indeed gather on the housetops, but

Sigurd greeted his mighty stepson without dismounting from his horse, and when the banqueting began, it was he and not Olaf who sat in the high seat. After all, it was *his* house!

On that occasion, to be sure, the cups and drinking horns were filled and filled again, but when Olaf stayed on for a week neither he nor his followers were feasted again.

"King Sigurd entertained them, day about, the one day with fish and milk, the other day with flesh meat and ale."

Even as recently as the last century, this was the common way of living among the peasants and the middle classes.

Sigurd was only a small ruler of a little region, but not even the mightiest monarchs of Denmark, Norway, and Sweden cared much more for pomp and circumstance, and even the most powerful of them recognized that they must have the support of their independent-minded people if they were to rule successfully.

Except for King Canute, the king of Denmark who also ruled Norway and England from 1016 to 1035, there were few in the Northland more powerful than Sverre Sigurdsson, who was king of Norway from 1184 to 1202.

Sverre came to power by the sword. To be sure, he claimed to be the son of a former king, but he could not mount the throne until his ragged army, called Birchlegs because the men were so poor they wore birch-bark trousers, had defeated and slain King Magnus.

But Sverre also wanted the people to approve of him.

"The King came to Nidaros [Trondheim]," says his historian, "and there he was received with the ringing of bells. He then caused a *thing* [a parliament to which all freemen could come] to be assembled, and this *thing* gave him the title of king. They ratified this by the clashing of swords."

Sword clashing was a custom to express approval which the Northmen inherited from their Germanic ancestors.

"After that land and liege were confirmed by oath in accordance with the old laws of the country."

Only then did Sverre feel entitled to rule.

This fundamental democracy—or maybe it would be better to say this innate belief that although there had to be a ruler, one man was as good as another, or almost so—is nowhere better illustrated than by the homes lived in by the men of these three classes.

One of the most famous of the buildings lived in by Northmen is described in the Anglo-Saxon poem, *Beowulf*. This is Heorot, or Hart Hall, the dwelling of King Hrothgar of the Danes. It had a golden roof-tree, its benches were plated with gold, and its walls were inlaid with ivory, but except for this magnificence, it could easily have been the abode of any powerful lord and it might even have belonged to a rich farmer. Let us consider a typical homestead of one of the latter.

In addition to its stone-walled fields, river and forest rights, and its summer mountain-pasture (*saeter*) complete with bleating goats and lowing cattle, a prosperous farm usually consisted of a group of buildings set about a principal farmhouse, or *skaale*.

Like Heorot, the *skaale* was often very imposing. "Tall and hightowering," it was generally rectangular in shape and sometimes was two hundred feet long. Although occasionally made of stone as thick as three feet, more often it was board and even log. The roof was steep to shed the snows and almost always was made of sturdy beams covered with birch bark over which sod was laid. It is a fact that flowers often grew in this sod in summer. There was a gable at either end, which was decorated either with antlers or a carved dragon's head.

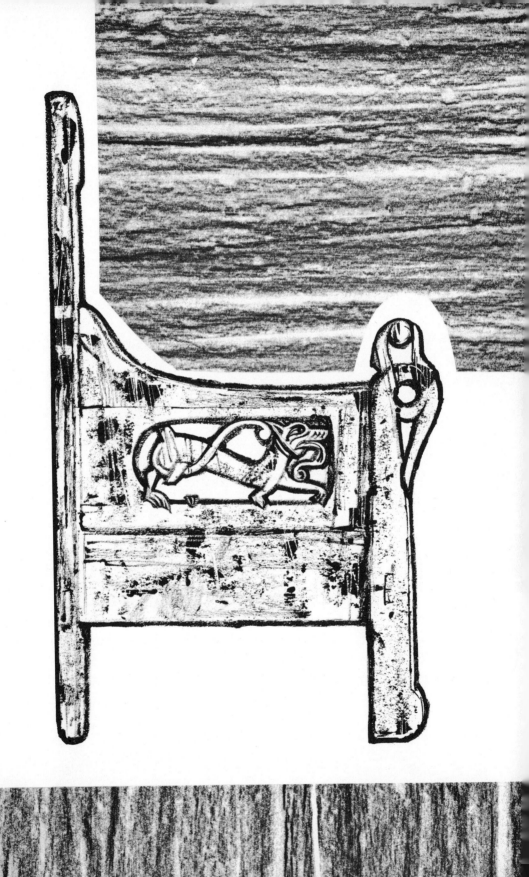

Most of the building was taken up by a main hall which ran from east to west, along the sides of which were fairly wide benches. In the center of one wall was the high seat for the head of the family or an honored guest. This high seat, as well as the posts which supported the walls, the door jambs, and even the walls themselves, were carved with intertwined animals—the so-called "gripping beast" style—or with plant scrolls or graceful leaf work.

Here, incidentally, we have an important example of Northman art, for the tillers of the Northmen's ships, their

sleds, their wagons, and even their beds, were similarly decorated, to say nothing of their pottery, the hilts of their
swords, their shields, their helmets, and all of their wonderful beakers, chalices, and cups. Woodcarving is still a Norwegian art.

In the middle of the room, there was a fireplace or a series
of fireplaces, and above them an opening through which the
smoke could escape. But most of it stayed in the room.

Farthest from the door was a bench for women. At its
corners were built-in beds. But most of the warriors and the
retainers slept on the benches. They simply rolled their cloaks
about themselves and stretched out.

The outbuildings varied from farm to farm, but those most
frequently found were the steward's house, the workshops,
the storehouses, the fish house, the boathouse, the brewhouse,
the weaving room, the stable, the smithy, the barn, and the
cowhouse. There was often a special house for maidservants
and a house for the master and his family.

Except when they were at their tasks and except for thralls
in their white wadmal, the Northmen, as they moved about
their home or rode to meetings or to a festival, were clad
resplendently. Here too their fundamental democracy was
evident. There was not much difference between a *karl* and a
king.

This, for example, is how a Norse chieftain dressed. Next
to his skin he wore a snugly fitting sark, or undershirt, and
over this a red or blue kirtle, or tunic. The latter was usually
sleeveless. About his waist he wore a broad leather belt
fastened by an ornate buckle. His trousers and his stockings
were frequently of one piece. His shoes resembled moccasins
but quite often they were laced about his calves.

When he went out, a cloak almost like a Roman toga was

thrown over his shoulders. It was fastened with a handsome pin. On his head he put a hat of wool felt—felt hats usually had no brim—sheepskin, fur, or even Oriental silk. The latter, shaped like turbans, were known as "Russian" hats.

His wife wore a long-sleeved garment—it was also called a kirtle—that trailed to the ground. Over this she sometimes wore an apron. Her stockings and her hose were probably embroidered. (Like Norse woodcarving, Norse embroidery is also famous even today.) The Norse women wore many kinds of headdress, but the most common was the *fald*. This was made of white linen and was very lofty. It resembled the headdress worn by Brittany peasants even in modern times. However, high-born women often wore a gold band or diadem.

Both men and women let their hair grow long, and the men were haughtily proud of their shoulder-length locks and of their golden beards and long mustaches. This pride is evidenced in some of the nicknames of Norse kings and chieftains: Harald Fairhair, Gold Harald, Svein Forkbeard, Sigtrygg Silkbeard. And when Njal, the wise old Icelander, was called "Old Beardless" by his enemies, his sons held this to be an insult which only blood could wipe out.

Both men and women wore jewelry, too, including earrings, arm rings, ankle rings, bracelets, pins, finger rings, and handsomely decorated tortoise-shaped thin metal plates known as bracteates. These were made of bronze, silver, and gold, but silver was the most highly esteemed. Indeed, jewelry was so important that when a gold ring given by King Olaf Tryggvason to Queen Sigrid the Haughty was found to be only gold-plated, she refused to become a Christian and to marry him. Thereupon he struck her in the face and called her an old heathen jade, thus setting into motion a train of events which finally led to his death.

As they wore this jewelry and these gaudy clothes, as they sat and slept in these halls, the Northmen developed a stirring way of living that has been described as "a strange blend of barbarism and culture."

From our point of view, for example, it was unbelievably cruel, although it must be remembered that in their day and age many other people were cruel too. But Northman cruelty was more than usually savage. In this respect, the Northmen were something like the American Indian. They tortured a vanquished foe, but they expected to be tortured themselves, and if they were, they stoically endured pain. To do otherwise would have been unmanly.

Even women were expected to endure torture. When Ethelred the Unready ordered the slaying of every Dane in England, he included the young and beautiful sister of Svein Forkbeard. He ordered his men to torture her fiendishly, but all she did was to laugh in the faces of her tormentors as they slew her.

As the vikings poured into an invaded town, they slaughtered men and women indiscriminately while they tossed little children from the points of their spears in fiendish sport. More barbarous than cruel, they sometimes cooked their food on spits stuck into the bodies of their fallen foes.

One viking chieftain even met a horrible death because of his savage ways. "Jarl Sigurd," reported a fellow Northman, "slew the Scotch lord, Melbridga Tunn, and then hung his head to his stirrup leather. But the calf of his leg was scratched by Melbridga's teeth and he died of blood poisoning."

Their religious practices were cruel as well, many of them being the same as those of their Stone Age ancestors. Human sacrifice, for instance, was carried out up to, and even after, the adoption of Christianity.

In 986, Jarl Hakon, then the ruler of Norway, fought a great battle with the Jömsvikings in a deep Norwegian fjord. Fortune began to turn against him.

Thereupon he went ashore on an island and prayed to the goddess Thorgerd Holgabrudr, but she was angry and would not hear him. He offered her sacrifices, and she refused them. Finally he offered his seven-year old son Erling.

She accepted Erling, and Hakon delivered him to his thrall Skopti, who killed him. Then the Jömsvikings fled.

This is not the only recorded case of human sacrifice among the Northmen although it is one of the latest. Indeed, it is said that in the very early days a Swedish tribe even went so far as to sacrifice their own local king during a period of severe famine. They sacrificed him to their tribal god of peace and plenty. Thereupon the grain began to ripen.

Like other Indo-Europeans, the Northmen worshiped many gods, some of which can be identified as forces of nature. The most important of these were the twelve Aesir.

Chief of the Aesir was Odin, after whom Wednesday (Odin's day) was named. Odin, according to Norse mythology, is the king of the gods. He has the rank of the Greek Zeus. But one of the sagas says that he came from Asia, which, according to it, is what Aesir means, and some scholars think that he was originally an Indo-European chieftain who led his people into Germany.

Odin had a gray beard and only one eye. His steed was called Sleipner. Sleipner had eight hoofs, could outrace the wind, and on one occasion galloped dry-shod over the sea as if it had been paved with stone.

Odin's principal wife was Frigg. (At least that is what most scholars think, but there is the goddess Freyja too, and this has caused some confusion). It is from "Frigg's day" that we get Friday. Frigg was the sky goddess, the goddess of marriage and of housewives. She was almost as wise as Odin and she did not always agree with him. When they quarreled she did not often come out the worst.

Another important Norse god was Thor. Thursday is named after him. As Donar he was worshiped by the ancient German tribes, some of whom considered him more powerful than Odin. Thor rode through the heavens in a mighty chariot drawn by two shaggy goats, and in his hand he held his magic hammer. (To the pagan Northmen, Thor's hammer had the same symbolic importance that the cross does to Christians.) When thunder rolled, the Northmen said that it was Thor's chariot. When an oak tree was split by a thunderbolt, they said that Thor had hurled his hammer at it. Thor's thirst was unquenchable, and according to the Northmen it was his thirst that gave them the tides. Twice a day Thor drained the sea through his drinking horn. Then it filled up again.

Besides the ones already named, there were many other gods. One was Tyr, after whom Tuesday is named. Tyr is represented as having only one hand, having thrust the other into the jaws of the evil wolf Fenris so that the Aesir could bind him. Tyr was sometimes thought of as the god of legal contracts.

Another god was the wicked Loki, who tricked the winter god Hod into slaying Balder with an arrow made of mistletoe. Balder was sent underground to the palace of Hel, but when all but one wicked old giantess wept for him, he was permitted to return to earth for six months of the year. That is why we have winter and summer.

Related to the gods were the Norns, three sisters who dwelt at the foot of the tree Yggdrasil. The Norns were almost the same as the Greek Fates. To newborn babes they came with lighted candles and determined their destiny. They even determined the destiny of the gods.

Most of these divine beings made their home in Asgard (the name means Aesir town) which is described as a celestial city filled with palaces and mansions almost like the great dwellings of the Norse kings and chieftains. Asgard was built by Odin himself. It was high in the heavens but was connected to the earth by Bifröst, the rainbow, down which the gods frequently came to visit the world. Indeed many of their adventures took place on earth, and in them they acted like human beings, eating and drinking, fighting, and often wooing lovely mortals. Sigurd—he is the Siegfried of Richard Wagner's operas—is said to be descended from one of Odin's sons.

The Norse gods were not immortal, and one day would come Ragnarok, which is better known as *Gotterdammerung*, or "the twilight of the gods." Then, through the hate of Fenris and the treachery of Loki, earth and heaven and all that lived in them would be destroyed. Odin would be destroyed in single-handed combat; Frigg would die of grief and shock; Thor would die as he slew the great serpent of Midgard; and finally Tyr would sink mortally wounded. After that the skies, scorched by fire giants, would split in two. The stars would fall into the void, and the earth would sink beneath the boiling water. The universe would be as it was before creation. Everything would come to an end.

In a way, there really was a twilight of the gods and it came sooner than was expected. Around 1000 A.D., the Norse countries became Christian.

This new faith was imposed by methods which were themselves savage and cruel. "I will lay waste the land and the islands if the people are not converted!" cried Olaf Tryggvason. And he kept his word.

He even surrounded a group of heathen leaders in their hall, and then he burned it down. House burning was often done by the Northmen. The practice was to get one's enemy in a house and then set fire to it. Women and children were usually invited to depart, but most of them preferred to stay with their husbands and fathers.

Olaf the Thick completed the conversion of the land in an equally savage manner. For clinging to the old ways, Olaf blinded King Raerik of Uppland and then led the poor king about in chains; and Olaf also had an earl murdered because the latter beat him at chess—and because the earl held to his pagan beliefs.

After that most of the northern lands at least paid lip service to the new religion.

But not even a royal decree, not even the sword and fire of King Olaf Tryggvason or of St. Olaf, could entirely wipe out the ancient faith. At any rate, not for quite a while. Nor could contact with other nations, which is really how Christianity first became known to the men of the North.

The merchant who traveled abroad might indeed find that it helped his business if he allowed himself to be *prime-signed,* that is, given a sort of preliminary baptism, which made him half a Christian but did not compel him to give up the old gods. The rich farmer and even the earl might deem it prudent to cross themselves and bow in prayer to "the white Christ"—this is what they called the Savior—if the king commanded. But in the beginning many, if not most, Northmen still clung secretly to the beliefs which they had held for more than two thousand years. Many of them continued to eat horseflesh, and some of them continued to "expose" (put out to die) unwanted children, practices forbidden to Christians. In their temples and sacred groves, the Northmen continued to practice heathen rites. In fact, for some time this was legal in Iceland. The very decree enacted in 1000 A.D. that made the island Christian permitted private worship of Odin and Thor.

When the Northmen were not savage, they were often barbaric. This is shown in their love of display, in their gold arm rings, and in their scarlet kirtles.

Their barbarism is also shown in at least one of their sports. The Northmen loved contests—they even had a word *idróttir,* which meant "skill in contests"—and these contests included not only mental exercises such as poetry reciting, saga reading, riddle solving, and chess or checker playing, but also wrestling, swimming, jumping, ball playing, snowshoe racing, spear throwing, arrow shooting, and fencing. The youthful Northman wished to excel in all.

But another Northman sport was horse fighting, and this was cruel. Two stallions were set against each other and goaded by their owners to fighting with their hoofs and teeth. It was almost certain that at least one of them would be killed in such a contest. Spectators, crowding the ring and betting heavily, were sometimes killed or injured too.

Last of all, feasts and festivals were wild and rude. The Northmen loved to entertain, and indeed in Iceland one chieftain set his home across the road so that travelers could not by-pass it, which was quite understandable. Life was lonely in the Northland, especially in winter when the roads were snow-choked and the nights never seemed to end. What could be more heartwarming than to see a party of horsemen moving toward you through the dusk? Now there would be new songs and stories, now there would be news. Almost more than any other people, the Northmen hungered for news.

But if these feasts were welcome, they often, perhaps

always, ended up as orgies. They usually lasted for at least three days, during which time ale, and sometimes mead, was passed from hand to hand and then passed back again until heads were dizzy. There were often drinking contests— "drinking by twins" this was called—and it was a breach of good manners to refuse either food or beverage offered to you by your host.

The Northmen enjoyed a wide variety of food. Besides the ever-present fish, they ate beef, mutton, horseflesh, eggs both from wild fowl and domestic poultry, milk and cheese, several kinds of cereals which they baked into flat bread like the modern Swedish bread or made into porridge, fruit, nuts, a few vegetables, and honey.

As can be imagined—in spite of the fact that the women, who took part in the drinking usually acted as peacemakers, throwing cloths or pieces of clothing over the fighters—the consequences were often disastrous. The Northman was quick of temper, and since swords were always handy, there was almost always bloodshed.

Yet, although he brawled or was brutal, the Northman displayed other highly admirable qualities, and to his credit were notable achievements.

First of all, he respected women, giving them a position which they never had again until modern times.

In most of medieval Europe, woman was the daughter of Eve, and since Eve had brought about the fall of man, she was thought of as being little better than the serpent. But among the Northmen, she was the companion of her husband. To be sure, a daughter, as well as a son, could be given in marriage by her father, but even at that her consent was considered necessary or at least advisable.

To be sure, a woman's husband was her legal guardian,

and only a widow had control of her own money and property and could do what she wanted with it without anyone else's approval.

To be sure, she was her man's housekeeper as well as his wife; if he was poor, she even milked his cows, fed and bedded his livestock, and helped in the hay making. Rich or poor, she kept his clothes in order, scrubbed him in his bath, and took off his garments when he was ready for bed. But even as he "ruled" her, or accepted her service, he made her, or she made herself, a partner in almost every important decision. In some matters she was the leader. For example, she was more apt to be concerned about family honor, and indeed a husband often risked death in battle to assure her he had defended it. "Never let my fair lady ever hear that I flinched!" cried one Northman as the swords leaped at him.

More than once, a woman even exerted national influence. The most famous instance is the case of King Harald Fairhair. As a young man, he was the king of only a few small districts, and at that time he sought to marry Gyda, the lovely daughter of King Eric of Rögaland.

"I will marry him only on condition that he makes himself king of the whole country!" Gyda said.

"That I will do," cried Harald, "and further I take the gods to witness that I will neither comb nor clip my hair until this is accomplished!"

That is how Norway came to be united, and how Harald got his name.

But respect for women was not the only enlightened characteristic of the Northman. Deep in his heart, too, was a love of personal freedom, a passion for justice, and a tremendous faith in legal procedures. Of the three characteristics, the last was perhaps the most notable.

No people since the Romans were so legal-minded as the Northmen, and this legal-minded way of looking at things was common not only to the warrior tugging at his oar, but also to the farmer ploughing his acres, both of whom could cite cases and precedents with fluency. For when you come right down to it, almost every Northman was a lawyer at heart. Very often he was what today we call "a Philadelphia lawyer," for technicalities were all-important!

This may come as a surprise, for most of us think of the Viking Age as a time when the sword settled everything, or if not the sword, an ordeal such as walking through fire or grasping a red-hot iron. But in the very days when *holmgang* —a duel fought on an island under very carefully drawn-up rules—was a national institution, even a murder could be settled at the end of a trial before the local parliament, or *thing,* by the payment of weregild, atonement money which was usually paid in the agreed number of ounces of silver.

(Incidentally, in such a trial, a man could be cleared by the sworn testimony of twelve "good and true" neighbors, a probable explanation of why English and American juries have twelve members, for this jury system was introduced to England by the Northmen.)

But law was not limited to rules concerning wounding and slaying. There were laws to cover almost everything from marriage and divorce to selling land or even cattle. There were even laws covering hospitality.

In Norway, the king frequently compelled his subjects to build guest shelters in lonely places, and in parts of Sweden country folk were required to supply travelers with food and their horses with fodder, the price being fixed by law. In Iceland, only bridal parties or persons journeying to a local or national *thing* had to be entertained this way. But here the penalty was lesser outlawry. A lesser outlaw had to live where he was told to and his relatives could visit him only once a month. If he broke bounds, he could be slain.

Finally, the Northmen contributed some of the most stirring poetry and prose that has ever been written.

Everyone has heard of the Norse sagas, the name of which comes from the *segin saga,* meaning "a tale told." Many people think that the sagas were poetry, but actually they were prose epics composed in accordance with strict rules, and halfway between history and a historical novel. In the beginning, they were recited at banquets by skilled storytellers known as "sagamen," many of whom could recite even the longest of these narratives without forgetting or changing a single word. Yet a saga recited to King Harald Hardraade took up twelve days of the Yuletide festival (incidentally, Yule as a name for Christmas comes from the Norse word for midwinter festival) before it was finished. It was not until after 1100 A.D. that any of them were written down.

The sagas were of many kinds. There were the historical sagas, of which the *Heimskringla* or "Chronicles of the Kings of Norway" is the most famous. This tells of the story of the rulers of Norway, legendary and real, from Odin who lived in the dim days of prehistory to Magnus Erlingsson who died in 1184. The *Heimskringla* is made up of eight individual sagas. In English it fills three large volumes.

Another kind of saga was the "family" saga. These told about the tragedies and the daily life of real people, who were not however kings or rulers. The best-known family saga is the *Njal's Saga* which tells about the venerable and wise old Njal and his friend Gunnar of Hlidarend, and their tangled fate which culminated in Njal's being burned in his Iceland farmhouse with his wife, his sons, and even a grandson.

There were also mythical and romantic sagas; ecclesiastical sagas which told about the lives of early bishops and priests; and sagas derived from Latin sources. Among the latter was the *Trojummanna saga,* or "Tale of the Trojans." Imagine that! Hector and Achilles celebrated by the Northmen! But these were relatively unimportant.

Most of the sagas were composed in Iceland and the most important writer of sagas was an Icelander, Snorri Sturluson. Snorri was a brawling political leader who was born in 1194 and died in 1241. Almost twenty-five years before

*Runestone*

Dante was born, over a century before Chaucer, and of course long before Shakespeare, this leader of a quarrelsome faction in the distant Arctic, amid his many other activities found time to take up his quill pen and set down one of the greatest books of all time. In those days, even in civilized Italy, most stories of the past were still dull and crabbed monkish chronicles. But the *Heimskringla* which Snorri wrote tells about men, some of whom were ancient even in Snorri's own time, so vividly that it is like reading about them in a daily newspaper.

The Northmen composed poetry too. In fact they composed poetry before they wrote prose. It is from ancient poetry that the writers of the sagas got much of their material.

The poetry was of two kinds—Eddaic and scaldic.

Eddaic poetry was older and more forthright in its style. To a great extent it dealt with heroes and gods. It was from the Eddas, for example, that Richard Wagner got the story of the Nibelungs, the theme for so many of his operas. But the Eddas also preserved the homely sayings of the *Hávamál,* one of which has already been given.

Scaldic poetry—called this because it was recited by scalds or professional poets who lived in the house of a great man or king—more often dealt with actual persons. Scaldic poetry is also noted for its elaborate figures of speech, which were called "kennings." In a kenning a sword was "the tongue of the scabbard," a spear "the wolf of the wound," a shield "the sun of the sea kings," the right arm "the falcon's seat," a ship "the reindeer of the deep," and the sea "the whale's bath." Kennings have gone out of fashion but some poets use them even today.

All these things—and especially Northman law and literature—should be remembered and balanced against the fire-gutted buildings on the Holy Island and elsewhere, and against the gold and other treasure carried off so high-handedly, to be buried underground; hoards, all glittering and golden, are uncovered frequently even today.

For the Northmen could build as well as destroy, a feature of their civilization which is particularly important to those of us who have an Anglo-Saxon heritage, for many of the institutions which we think of as having an Anglo-Saxon origin really have come from the Northmen. For example, we live under a government by parliament or congress, and when I went to school we were taught that this came from the Anglo-Saxon *witenagemot,* or council of the king's wise men. But much more like out present-day legislative bodies was the Iceland *Althing,* founded in 930 and still in existence. It is the oldest parliamentary body in the world.

(Our very term "Speaker of the House" or "Speaker of Parliament," used to denote presiding officers of our House of Representatives and England's Parliament, comes from the *Althing* whose presiding officer was known as the lawspeaker.)

We live in a world of law, but the very word "law" comes from the Norse *log.* The Anglo-Saxon word was *dom,* our "doom."

And we also get from the Northmen, who settled half of England and intermingled with the Anglo-Saxons, that combination of clear-sighted fair-mindedness and courage mingled with a sense of adventure which has carried the descendants of these northern races all over the globe, and which, in spite of a fair amount of Norse stubbornness, has enabled them to leave almost every place they came to a little better (and often a lot better) than it was before.

# The Northmen Later
# and Today

The Viking Age began at about the time of the attack on
Lindisfarne. Authorities do not agree as to just when it ended.

Some say that it was when St. Olaf was defeated in the battle
of Stiklestad. This was fought in 1030 during a total eclipse
on a hillside forty miles north of Trondheim.

After an earlier defeat Olaf, who had angered the heathen
farmers by forcing them to become Christian, had fled to
Russia. But now, wearing a golden helmet, carrying a white
shield with a golden cross, and wielding a sword called "the
Slicer," he marched back over the "keel" of Norway—the
ridge which divides Norway from Sweden—with 3,600 men.

At least three times as many of the farmer-landowners
awaited him. They were in the pay of King Canute of England and Denmark, and were led by Thorer Hund, Kalf
Arneson, and Thorstein Knararsmed, the latter said to be "a
merchant, a master ship carpenter, and a great manslayer."

But Olaf and his followers were undaunted.

"*Fram, fram, Kristsmenn, krossmenn, konungsmenn!*" they shouted. "Forward, Christ's men, Cross men, King's men!"

Arrows darkened the air and Olaf himself cut down enemy after enemy. At last he was surrounded, however, and Thorer Hund, wearing a reindeer-skin coat, which he said had been rendered wound-proof by Lapland magic, thrust a spear through Olaf's coat of mail.

Olaf then staggered to a huge boulder, leaned against it, and expired. After that the Norwegians were too busy with strife at home to take part in many foreign adventures.

Others say that the Viking Age ended in 1042 when Danish Hardecanute, King Canute's weak son, died, and the throne of England went back to an Englishman with Northman blood, Edward the Confessor.

By that time Northman rule had been ended in Ireland. The Scandinavian rulers had become Slavic. The Northmen of Normandy (Normans) had become at least half French. In Iceland, blood feuds between the great families had become so violent that in 1262, the island, torn by internal disorders, had to submit to Norway. Greenland, the most distant outpost of the Northmen, would soon be forgotten in the increasing Arctic cold.

But there are others who hold that the last manifestation of the Viking Age was the Crusades, which began in 1096 and ended in 1272.

Some people, pointed out the historian Sir Steven Runciman, think of the Crusades "as the most tremendous and romantic of Christian adventures," but they may just as well have been "the last of the barbarian invasions."

There is much to be said for this last point of view, for although crusaders said that their purpose was to redeem the Holy Land, quite often they were little better than piratical robbers.

There were, too, many Northmen who took part in the Crusades, the most renowned being King Sigurd the Jerusalem-farer. The most romantic of all crusaders, Richard the Lion-Hearted, King of England, was descended from a Norwegian. He was the eighth-generation descendant of the viking chieftain Rögnvald of Möre, the first Northman jarl of Orkney.

But whenever the Viking Age did end, after that we hear relatively little of these northerners. They had sailed half the world, but now they withdrew to Scandinavia, where they were not vikings any more, or even Northmen, but Danes, Swedes, and Norwegians, gradually developing into the people we know today.

This does not mean that they had no history or that the history they had was uneventful. Very far from it! And at least once one of the Northman countries had a brief return to national glory.

In the sixteenth century, Sweden was ruled tyranically by Denmark's cruel King Christian II—"a fine beast if he only knew Latin" is how a pope described him—and in 1520, the Swedes revolted.

Christian immediately invaded their land, defeated the rebels, and in spite of pleas for mercy—some even from his own courtiers—executed ninety Swedish leaders on a black day which is still known as "the Stockholm blood bath."

One of the executed leaders was Eric Johannson, a Swedish nobleman who had a chance to escape but refused. "I will in God's name die rather with my brothers, all honorable men!" he cried.

He did die, but his son was the famous Gustavus Vasa who freed Sweden and founded the Vasa dynasty which ruled for almost three hundred years. Under Gustavus and his successors, Sweden became the most important power in the eastern Baltic and indeed in northern Europe.

The Vasas not only ruled almost all of present-day Sweden, but Finland, Estonia, Livonia (part of prewar Latvia), Ingria (the land around Leningrad), and Courland (part of prewar Latvia and prewar Lithuania). They only began losing these lands after Charles XII (1697–1718)—he too was a brilliant general, but he was rash and foolish—marched halfway across Russia to do battle with Peter the Great near the banks of the Dneister.

He was defeated at Poltava in the Ukraine and fled to the Turks.

After that, as Denmark and Norway already had, Sweden became a second-rate power. The grandeur of the Scandinavian people seemed finally ended.

Now, however, we are hearing of the Northmen again and in a very different fashion.

"Scandinavia is one of the wonders of the modern world," writes an American geographer. "Located in almost precisely the same latitude as Alaska, consisting largely of mountainous country unsuited for agriculture, and poorly endowed, this land has produced one of the most advanced cultures in history."

It is not merely that they have supported themselves—and even made themselves at least moderately prosperous—in a difficult climate.

This, of course, they have certainly done.

Little Denmark, for example, is one of the most successful farming countries in the world. It not only feeds itself, but it sends large amounts of bacon, eggs, and butter to the breakfast tables of England, Sweden, and France. It is one of the few countries where the farmers have brought wealth to the country as a whole.

The Swedes are noted for their steel products, including the ships they build, and for their excellent glassware, pottery, and silverware. These too have been exported extensively, enabling the Swedes to purchase many things they cannot produce themselves. The Swedes are noted for their good living.

The Norwegians have gone back to the sea. Norway has the fourth largest merchant marine in the world—in tonnage almost half as large as that of the United States or of the United Kingdom. Today the viking ships of old have been replaced by sturdy little tramp steamers which chug the seven seas as they carry the world's cargoes. But there are also Norwegian trawlers operating in the chilliest of northern waters and a fleet of modern whalers which sail to the Antarctic.

Kept from anything but the most rudimentary farming by their short bleak summer and their long winter, the Icelanders make their living from trout, salmon, herring, halibut, and cod.

But even as they do this, the people of the North also have time for things of the spirit.

Even today, the total population of the four Norse countries is less than sixteen million, yet in relatively recent times they have produced an array of artists, authors, and musicians that would bring pride to any country. Hans Christian Andersen, the storyteller. The playwrights, Henrik Ibsen and August Strindberg. The novelists, Knut Hamsun, Sigrid Undset, and Selma Lagerlöf. The composer Grieg. And, of course, many more.

In architecture, particularly modern architecture, and

home furnishings the Scandinavians are equally outstanding. Stockholm and Copenhagen are considered to be among the world's most beautiful cities.

They also have distinguished themselves in science and with their inventions. An inventor particularly important to the United States is John Ericsson, a Swede who invented the iron-clad warship. It was his *Monitor* which, during the Civil War, saved the American Navy. He invented the screw propeller too. Alfred Nobel invented dynamite—and with the proceeds endowed the Nobel prizes, including the Nobel Peace prize.

Many of the sons of the Northmen have won Nobel prizes themselves—in physics, in chemistry, and in physiology and medicine as well as in literature.

Most famous of these was Niels Bohr, a Dane. Bohr laid the foundations for what is known as the "quantum theory of matter," and he was the first one to find out how the atom was put together and how it could be taken apart. For this he won the Nobel prize in 1922.

He not only made possible the atom bomb, but, escaping from occupied Denmark, he warned the Allies that the Germans would soon have one too. He also warned of the dangers of using this weapon.

The new Northmen have also pioneered in social consciousness, and it is here that we have most reason to be grateful to them. Their educational system is second to none, and they were among the first to provide social-welfare programs including old-age pensions, maternity benefits, family allowances, health insurance, workman's-compensation insurance, and unemployment insurance. These are all state supported and they do not seem to have destroyed individual initiative.

Whether they will work in another country is something we can argue about, but they certainly work in Norway, Denmark, and Sweden.

Last of all, and perhaps most surprising, these descendants of the ancient vikings have worked for and have made many contributions to the cause of world peace. Following World War I, Fridtjof Nansen, the Arctic explorer serving as the League of Nations' high commissioner for refugees, saved literally millions of refugees from death or misery. It was he who invented the so-called Nansen passport which could be used by people who, because of the war, no longer had a country.

But since World War II, the contributions have been even more notable. The first two secretaries of the United Nations were sons of the ancient Northmen. They even had viking names. Trygve (Trygve was the father of Olaf Tryggvason) Lie, and Dag (there was a legendary Swedish king, Dag) Hammarskjöld. Swedish Count Folke Bernadotte, who was murdered as he tried to make peace between the Jews and the Arabs, was also a Northman who worked for peace. All three are now world heroes.

The first time we saw the Northman, he was leaping ashore, sword in hand, at the holy island of Lindisfarne. But now Northmen are using their courage, their sense of justice, and their belief in law for the benefit of all humanity. They are setting an example to the whole world.

# Chronological Chart
## of the Northmen
## and World Events

| | NORTHMEN'S WORLD | ENGLAND AND WESTERN EUROPE |
|---|---|---|
| A.D. 300–400 | | Visigoths defeat and slay Roman emperor, 376; pour into Balkans; cross Danube and Rhine |
| 400–500 | | St. Patrick sent to convert Irish, 432; establishes monastic orders in Ireland. Columba and Augustine convert Scotch and English 100 years later |
| | | Visigoths and Vandals sack Rome; last Roman emperor deposed, 476 |
| | | First Saxon kingdom in Britain, 477; Clovis I founds Frank kingdom in France, 481 |
| 500–600 | Hygelac, king of Danish Geats (described in Beowulf), raids tribes in Lowlands (Holland), 521 | |
| 600–700 | | |
| 700–800 | First Northman invasions of England, Ireland, and Continent: Northmen anchor off island of Eigg in Scotch Hebrides and Tory Island near Ireland, before 700 Lindisfarne destroyed, 793 First raids against Ireland, 795 Attacks launched against Frisland (Holland), around 800 Charlemagne's realm in France invaded, 810 | Charles Martel defeats Moslems at Tours, France, 732; stops Arab expansion in Europe Charlemagne mounts Frankish throne, 768; crowned emperor of Holy Roman Empire at Rome, 800 |
| 800–900 | Viking centers established at York in England; Dublin, Waterford, and Limerick in Ireland; Shetland Islands, Hebrides, Orkneys, and Faeroes | |
| | | Vikings attack in the Baltic as far as modern-day Leningrad; Hamburg burned 851 and 880 |
| | Norwegians discover Iceland, 861; begin settlement, 875 | Vikings attack in the Mediterranean, 859; travel as far as Palestine; perhaps see Constantinople as Varangians approach across Black Sea |
| | | Vikings plunder major cities in France (Rouen, Nantes, Bordeaux, Toulouse, Orléans, etc.); Paris besieged, 885 |
| | Alfred the Great forces Danish Vikings to withdraw from England, 897 | |
| 900–1000 | Harald Fairhair unites Norway, about 900 | Arab rule in Spain at height; Cordova greatest intellectual center in Western Europe |

| | NEAR EAST AND ASIA | WESTERN HEMISPHERE |
|---|---|---|
| **A.D.** 300–400 | | *Maya period of prosperity, 300–700* |
| 400–500 | | |
| 500–600 | | |
| 600–700 | *Beginnings of Arab Empire, 632; Arabs conquer Persia, Egypt, North Africa, Spain* | |
| 700–800 | *Golden Age of Arab Empire under Abbasid dynasty, 750–1258* | |
| 800–900 | | |
| | Varangians (Swedes) travel south and east as far as Baghdad; attack Constantinople 860, 941, and 944<br><br>Rurik founds viking state at Novgorod, 862<br><br>*Byzantine civilization advances greatly under Macedonian dynasty, 867–1056* | |
| 900–1000 | | |

| | NORTHMEN'S WORLD | ENGLAND AND WESTERN EUROPE |
|---|---|---|
| **A.D.** 900–1000 | | A Northman invader (Rollo) made first duke of Normandy by Charles the Simple of France, 911; attacks in northern France end |
| | Althing (national assembly) founded in Iceland, 930 Olaf Tryggvason, 969–1000, famous warrior and king of Norway St. Olaf, 995–1030, patron saint of Norway Beginnings of Northman literature, the *Eddas*, composed between tenth and thirteenth centuries | |
| 1000–1100 | Most Northmen adopt Christianity by 1000 | |
| | Brian Boru, king of Ireland, breaks Northman rule in Ireland in Battle of Clontarf, 1014 | |
| | Harald Hardraade, 1015–1066, ruler of Norway and adventurer in Mediterranean and Byzantine East; hero of many sagas | |
| | England, Denmark, and Norway ruled by Canute the Great, from 1016–1035 | |
| | | *William the Conqueror invades England, 1066* |
| 1100–1200 | | Roger II, son of a Norman conqueror, made king of Sicily, 1130 |
| | Vikings reach Spitsbergen in Arctic Circle, 1194 Snorri Sturluson (an Icelander) writes *Heimskringla*, 1194–1241 | |
| 1200–1300 | | *Magna Charta in England, 1215* |
| 1300–1400 | | |
| 1400–1500 | | *Moors expelled from Spain: Beginning of Spanish explorations of New World* *Invention of printing, 1439* |

# Northmen and World Events

| | NEAR EAST AND ASIA | WESTERN HEMISPHERE |
|---|---|---|
| **A.D.**<br>900–1000 | Varangians take Baku and march to Azerbaijan, 912 | |
| 1000–1100 | | Bjarni Herjulfson, a Norwegian, probably sails to New World, 985<br>Eric the Red explores Greenland; founds colony, 986<br>Leif Ericsson visits Newfoundland, Nova Scotia, Vinland, 999 |
| 1100–1200 | *Seljuk Turks seize Baghdad, 1055; defeat Byzantines in Armenia, 1071 (decline of Byzantine military power)*<br>*Crusades against Moslems in Holy Lands, 1096–1270*<br>King Sigurd the Jerusalemfarer, a famous Northman, goes on Crusade, 1107–1111 | |
| 1200–1300 | | |
| 1300–1400 | *Genghis Khan conquers central Asia and China, 1206–1221; Mongols overthrow Arab Empire, 1258*<br>*Ottoman Empire (Turks) founded, 1288*<br>*Tamerlane ruler of Asia from Russia to Persian Gulf, 1369–1405* | |
| 1400–1500 | *Ottoman Turks invade Europe, defeat Serbs, 1389; overthrow Byzantine Empire, 1453* | *Rise of Aztec civilization*<br><br>*Columbus discovers America, 1492* |

# Books for
# Further Reading
# and Index

# Books for Further Reading

*The Anglo-Saxon Chronicle,* trans. with introduction by G. N. Garmonsway. New York, E. P. Dutton and Company, Inc., 1953

Arbmann, Holger, *The Vikings.* New York, Frederick A. Praeger, Inc., 1961

Berry, Erick, *The King's Jewel.* New York, The Viking Press, 1957

Best, Herbert, *The Sea Warriors.* New York, The Macmillan Company, 1959

Blake, N. F., trans., *The Saga of the Jomsvikings.* New York, Thomas Nelson & Sons, 1962

Boucher, Alan, *Sea Warriors and Dragon Ships* (with Alan French's *Rolf and the Viking Bow*). New York, Walker and Company, 1963

Coblentz, Catherine, *The Falcon of Eric the Red.* New York, Longmans, Green, 1942

Colum, Padriac, *The Children of Odin: The Book of Northern Myths.* New York, The Macmillan Company, 1962

French, Alan, *Rolf and the Viking Bow* (with Alan Boucher's *Sea Warriors and Dragon Ships*). New York, Walker and Company, 1963

Hangaard, Erik Christian, *Hakon of Rogen's Saga.* Boston, Houghton Mifflin Company, 1963

Hollander, Lee M., ed., *Saga of the Jomsvikings.* Austin, University of Texas, 1955

——, trans., *The Poetic Edda,* 3rd revised ed. Austin, University of Texas, 1962

Hollander, Lee M., and Bayerschmidst, Carl F., trans. *Njal's Saga*. New York, New York University Press, 1955.

Hull, Eleanor, *The Northmen in Britain*. New York, Thomas Y. Crowell Company, 1913

Janeway, Elizabeth, *The Vikings* (biography of Leif Ericsson). New York, Random House, 1951

Kendrick, T. D., *Late Saxon and Viking Art*. New York, Humanities Press, 1949

Leighton, Margaret, *Journey for a Princess*. New York, Farrar, Straus, 1960

Longfellow, Henry Wadsworth, "The Saga of King Olaf" in *Tales of a Wayside Inn*. New York, David McKay Company, Inc., 1961

Polland, Madeleine A., *Beorn the Proud*. New York, Holt, Rinehart and Winston, 1962

Resnick, William S., *The Dragon Ship, A Story of the Vikings in America*. New York, Coward McCann, Inc., 1942.

Roberts, Dorothy, *Fire in the Ice*. Boston, Little, Brown, 1961

Sutcliff, Rosemary, *Shield Ring*. New York, Oxford University Press, 1957

——, ed. *Beowulf*. New York, E. P. Dutton and Company, 1962

Treece, Henry, *The Road to Miklagard*. New York, Criterion Books, 1957

——, *Viking's Dawn*. New York, Criterion Books, 1956

——, *Viking's Sunset*. New York, Criterion Books, 1960

# Index

# ABOUT THE AUTHOR

THOMAS CALDECOT CHUBB, internationally known author, scholar, and literary critic, began his writing career while still a student at Yale with the publication of two books, one of which won him the Albert Stanborough Cook award for poetry, and a poem which won him the John Masefield Award. Since that time he has published a number of books which are outstanding for both scholarship and writing—among these his well-known biography *Aretino: Scourge of Princes* for adults, *The Byzantines,* selected by the American Library Association as a Notable Book of the Year, 1959, and *Slavic Peoples.*

World traveler, sportsman, and civic leader, Mr. Chubb and his wife now divide their time between Connecticut and Georgia.

2  3  4  5  68  67  66